DATE DUE

Creation of the Modern Middle East

Saudi Arabia

Creation of the Modern Middle East

Saudi
Arabia

Heather Lehr Wagner

Introduction by
Akbar Ahmed
School of International Service
American University

CHELSEA HOUSE
P U B L I S H E R S
A Haights Cross Communications Company
Philadelphia

Frontispiece: Ibn Saud Abdul Aziz with brothers and sons, March 11, 1911

Cover: Sunlight on Masjid an-Nabawi in Medina.

CHELSEA HOUSE PUBLISHERS

VP, NEW PRODUCT DEVELOPMENT Sally Cheney
DIRECTOR OF PRODUCTION Kim Shinners
CREATIVE MANAGER Takeshi Takahashi
MANUFACTURING MANAGER Diann Grasse

Staff for SAUDI ARABIA

EDITOR Lee Marcott
PRODUCTION EDITOR Jaimie Winkler
PICTURE RESEARCHER Sarah Bloom
SERIES AND COVER DESIGNER Keith Trego
LAYOUT 21st Century Publishing and Communications, Inc.

3 5 7 9 8 6 4 2

Library of Congress Cataloging-in-Publication Data applied for.

ISBN 0-7910-6510-3

Table of Contents

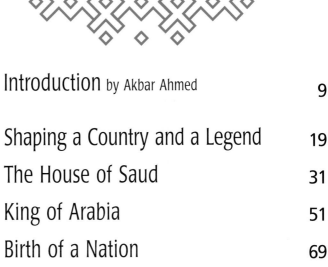

Index to the Photographs

Creation of the Modern Middle East

Iran

Iraq

Israel

Jordan

The Kurds

Kuwait

Oman

Palestinian Authority

Saudi Arabia

Syria

Turkey

Yemen

Introduction

Akbar Ahmed

The Middle East, it seems, is always in the news. Unfortunately, most of the news is of a troubling kind. Stories of suicide bombers, hijackers, street demonstrations, and ongoing violent conflict dominate these reports. The conflict draws in people living in lands far from the Middle East; some support one group, some support another, often on the basis of kinship or affinity and not on the merits of the case.

The Middle East is often identified with the Arabs. The region is seen as peopled by Arabs speaking Arabic and belonging to the Islamic faith. The stereotype of the Arab oil sheikh is a part of contemporary culture. But both of these images—that the Middle East is in perpetual anarchy and that it has an exclusive Arab identity—are oversimplifications of the region's complex contemporary reality.

In reality, the Middle East is an area that straddles Africa and Asia and has a combined population of over 200 million people inhabiting over twenty countries. It is a region that draws the entire world into its politics and, above all, it is the land that is the birth place of the three great Abrahamic faiths—Judaism, Christianity, and Islam. The city of Jerusalem is the point at which these three faiths come together and also where they tragically confront one another.

It is for these reasons that knowledge of the Middle East will remain of importance and that news from it will remain ongoing and interesting.

Let us consider the stereotype of the Middle East as a land of constant anarchy. It is easy to forget that some of the greatest lawgivers and people of peace were born, lived, and died here. In the Abrahamic tradition these names are a glorious roll call of human history—Abraham, Moses, Jesus, and Muhammad. In the tradition of the Middle East, where these names are especially revered, people often add the blessing "Peace be upon him" when speaking their names.

The land is clearly one that is shared by the great faiths. While it has a dominant Muslim character because of the large Muslim population, its Jewish and Christian presence must not be underestimated. Indeed, it is the dynamics of the relationships between the three faiths that allow us to enter the Middle East today and appreciate the points where these faiths come together or are in conflict.

To understand the predicament in which the people of the Middle East find themselves today, it is well to keep the facts of history before us. History is never far from the minds of the people in this region. Memories of the first great Arab dynasty, the Umayyads (661-750), based in Damascus, and the even greater one of the Abbasids (750-1258), based in Baghdad, are still kept alive in books and folklore. For the Arabs, their history, their culture, their tradition, their language, and above all their religion, provide them with a rich source of pride; but the glory of the past contrasts with the reality and powerlessness of contemporary life.

Many Arabs have blamed past rulers for their current situation beginning with the Ottomans who ruled them until World War I and then the European powers that divided their lands. When they achieved independence after World War II they discovered that the artificial boundaries created by the European powers cut across tribes and clans. Today, too, they complain that a form of Western imperialism still dominates their politics and rulers.

Again, while it is true that Arab history and Arab temperament have colored the Middle East strongly, there are other distinct peoples who have made a significant contribution to the culture of the region. Turkey is one such non-Arab nation with its own language, culture, and contribution to the region through the influence of the Ottoman Empire. Memories of that period for the Arabs are mixed, but what cannot be denied are the spectacular administrative and architectural achievements of the Ottomans. It is the longest dynasty in world history, beginning in 1300 and ending after World War I in 1922, when Kemal Ataturk wished to reject the past on the way to creating a modern Turkey.

Similarly, Iran is another non-Arab country with its own rich language and culture. Based in the minority sect of Islam, the Shia, Iran has often been in opposition to its Sunni neighbors, both Arab and Turk. Perhaps this confrontation helped to forge a unique Iranian, or Persian, cultural identity that, in turn, created the brilliant art, architecture, and poetry under the Safawids (1501-1722). The Safawid period also saw the establishment of the principle of interference or participation—depending on one's perspective—in matters of the state by the religious clerics. So while the Ayatollah Khomeini was very much a late 20th century figure, he was nonetheless reflecting the patterns of Iranian history.

Israel, too, represents an ancient, non-Arabic, cultural and religious tradition. Indeed, its very name is linked to the tribes that figure prominently in the stories of the Bible and it is through Jewish tradition that memory of the great biblical patriarchs like Abraham and Moses is kept alive. History is not a matter of years, but of millennia, in the Middle East.

Perhaps nothing has evoked as much emotional and political controversy among the Arabs as the creation of the state of Israel in 1948. With it came ideas of democracy and modern culture that seemed alien to many Arabs. Many saw the wars that followed stir further conflict and hatred; they also saw the wars as an inevitable clash between Islam and Judaism.

It is therefore important to make a comment on Islam and Judaism. The roots of prejudice against Jews can be anti-Semitic, anti-Judaic, and anti-Zionist. The prejudice may combine all three and there is often a degree of overlap. But in the case of the Arabs, the matter is more complicated because, by definition, Arabs cannot be anti-Semitic because they themselves are considered Semites. They cannot be anti-Judaic, because Islam recognizes the Jews as "people of the Book."

What this leaves us with is the clash between the political philosophy of Zionism, which is the establishment of a Jewish nation in Palestine, and Arab thought. The antagonism of the Arabs to Israel may result in the blurring of lines. A way must be found by Arabs and Israelis to live side by side in peace. Perhaps recognition of the common Abrahamic tradition is one way forward.

The hostility to Israel partly explains the negative coverage the Arabs get in the Western media. Arab Muslims are often accused of being anarchic and barbaric due to the violence of the Middle East. Yet, their history has produced some of the greatest figures in history.

Consider the example of Sultan Salahuddin Ayyoubi, popularly called Saladin in Western literature. Saladin had vowed to take revenge for the bloody massacres that the Crusaders had indulged in when they took Jerusalem in 1099. According to a European eyewitness account the blood in the streets was so deep that it came up to the knees of the horsemen.

Yet, when Saladin took Jerusalem in 1187, he showed the essential compassion and tolerance that is at the heart of the Abrahamic faiths. He not only released the prisoners after ransom, as was the custom, but paid for those who were too poor to afford any ransom. His nobles and commanders were furious that he had not taken a bloody revenge. Saladin is still remembered in the bazaars and villages as a leader of great learning and compassion. When contemporary leaders are compared to Saladin, they are usually found wanting. One reason may be that the problems of the region are daunting.

The Middle East faces three major problems that will need solutions in the twenty-first century. These problems affect society and politics and need to be tackled by the rulers in those lands and all other people interested in creating a degree of dialogue and participation.

The first of the problems is that of democracy. Although democracy is practiced in some form in a number of the Arab countries, for the majority of ordinary people there is little sense of participation in their government. The frustration of helplessness in the face of an indifferent bureaucracy at the lower levels of administration is easily converted to violence. The indifference of the state to the pressing needs of the "street" means that other non-governmental organizations can step in. Islamic organizations offering health and education programs to people in the shantytowns and villages have therefore emerged and flourished over the last decades.

The lack of democracy also means that the ruler becomes remote and autocratic over time as he consolidates his power. It is not uncommon for many rulers in the Middle East to pass on their rule to their son. Dynastic rule, whether kingly or based in a dictatorship, excludes ordinary people from a sense of participation in their own governance. They need to feel empowered. Muslims need to feel that they are able to participate in the process of government. They must feel that they are able to elect their leaders into office and if these leaders do not deliver on their promises, that they can throw them out. Too many of the rulers are nasty and brutish. Too many Muslim leaders are kings and military dictators. Many of them ensure that their sons or relatives stay on to perpetuate their dynastic rule.

With democracy, Muslim peoples will be able to better bridge the gaps that are widening between the rich and the poor. The sight of palatial mansions with security guards carrying automatic weapons standing outside them and, alongside, hovels teeming with starkly poor children is a common one in Muslim cities. The distribution of wealth must remain a priority of any democratic government.

The second problem in the Middle East that has wide ramifications in society is that of education. Although Islam emphasizes knowledge and learning, the sad reality is that the standards of education are unsatisfactory. In addition, the climate for scholarship and intellectual activity is discouraging. Scholars are too often silenced, jailed, or chased out of the country by the administration. The sycophants and the intelligence services whose only aim is to tell the ruler what he would like to hear, fill the vacuum.

Education needs to be vigorously reformed. The *madrassah,* or religious school, which is the institution that provides primary education for millions of boys in the Middle East, needs to be brought into line with the more prestigious Westernized schools reserved for the elite of the land. By allowing two distinct streams of education to develop, Muslim nations are encouraging the growth of two separate societies: a largely illiterate and frustrated population that is susceptible to leaders with simple answers to the world's problems and a small, Westernized, often corrupt and usually uncaring group of elite. The third problem facing the Middle East is that of representation in the mass media. Although this point is hard to pin down, the images in the media are creating problems of understanding and communication in the communities living in the Middle East. Muslims, for example, will always complain that they are depicted in negative stereotypes in the non-Arab media. The result of the media onslaught that plagues Muslims is the sense of anger on the one hand and the feeling of loss of dignity on the other. Few Muslims will discuss the media rationally. Greater Muslim participation in the media and greater interaction will help to solve the problem. But it is not so simple. The Israelis also complain of the stereotypes in the Arab media that depict them negatively.

Muslims are aware that their religious culture represents a civilization rich in compassion and tolerance. They are aware that given a period of stability in which they can grapple with the problems of democracy, education, and self-image they can take their rightful place in the community of nations. However painful the current reality, they do carry an idea of an ideal human society with them. Whether a Turk, or an Iranian, or an Arab, every Muslim is aware of the message that the prophet of Islam brought to this region in the seventh century. This message still has resonance for these societies. Here are words from the last address of the prophet spoken to his people:

> All of you descend from Adam and Adam was made of earth. There is no superiority for an Arab over a non-Arab nor for a non-Arab over an Arab, neither for a white man over a black man nor a black man over a white man . . . the noblest among you is the one who is most deeply conscious of God.

This is a noble and worthy message for the twenty-first century in the Middle East. Not only Muslims, but Jews, and Christians would agree with it. Perhaps its essential theme of tolerance, compassion, and equality can help to rediscover the wellsprings of tradition that can both inspire and unite.

It is for these reasons that I congratulate Chelsea House Publishers for taking the initiative in helping us to understand the Middle East through this series. The story of the Middle East is, in many profound ways, the story of human civilization.

— **Dr. Akbar S. Ahmed**
The Ibn Khaldun Chair of Islamic Studies and
Professor of International Relations,
School of International Service
American University

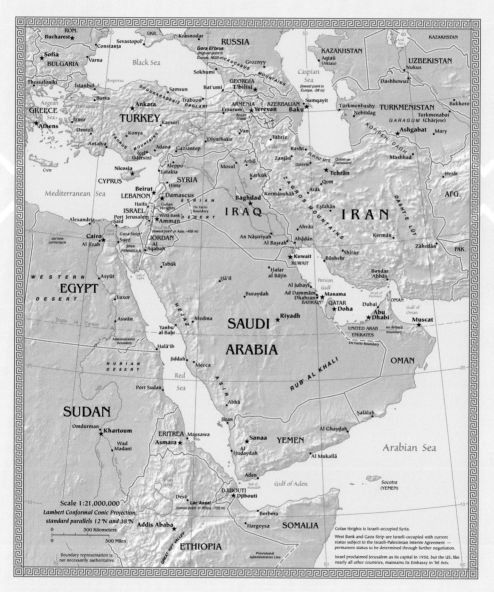

Map of the Middle East region

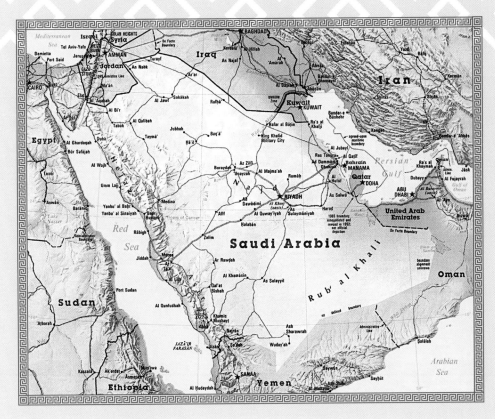

Modern map of Saudi Arabia

The Ka'ba, c. 1884–89

This is among the earliest photographs of the Ka'ba.

Al-Sayyid Abd al-Ghaffar, considered the earliest Arabian photographer, sent his original photographic plate to C. Snouck Hurgronje, former Netherlands Consul in Jiddah. It appears, without the elaborate calligraphed signatures, in Snouck's volume *Bilder aus Mekka* (1889).

The Ka'ba is considered by Muslims everywhere to be the most sacred spot on Earth. Located in the Ka'ba is the stone Muslims believe was given to Adam on his expulsion from Paradise. Originally white, the stone has become black by absorbing the sins of the pilgrims who have touched it.

1

Shaping a Country
and a Legend

On October 30, 1918, a young British colonel was given the rare honor of a private meeting with his king. King George V had agreed to the meeting in part out of curiosity. The young colonel, T.E. Lawrence, had gained a reputation for obtaining strategically important information in the critical area of the world we know today as the Middle East. Lawrence had proven himself particularly skillful at dealing with the Arabs who populated the region, and had been able to provide British forces with details of key supply routes and to muster Arab support during some of the fiercest fighting of World War I.

But it was not only his expertise in the people and geography of the region that had made his reputation. Lawrence shunned the traditional British uniform of khakis and sun hats. Instead, he clothed himself in Arab robes, an astonishing image to both Europeans and Arabs alike in his flowing white silk and gold-embroidered outfits. His wild exploits and skillful self-promotion had guaranteed that his reputation preceded him as he was presented to the King.

The meeting had been arranged, at least in part, as a way to honor Lawrence for his service during the war. He was to have been appointed a Commander of the Bath, an honor recognizing his outstanding military accomplishments. As the King prepared to remove the medal from its cushion and present it to the young colonel, Lawrence stopped him. He could not, he explained, accept the award, for he believed that the role he had played on behalf of the British government was not an honorable one. He expressed his dismay that the British government had, through him and via other channels, made a series of false promises to the Arab people, and indicated that he now felt it was his duty to his Arab friends to join their struggle to regain the territory that had been promised them.

It was an astonishing scene, and one that deeply displeased the King: a member of his own military declining a prestigious medal and, instead, expressing his disagreement with British policies in the region from where he had only recently returned. But for those familiar with Lawrence, it was merely the latest chapter in a controversial and unpredictable life.

The tales of Lawrence's exploits in the Middle East would make him a celebrity. His outspokenness would make him a thorn in the side of British officials, who desperately wanted to exploit his connections and information while downplaying his significance to their efforts in the region. The man who would become known as "Lawrence of Arabia" shaped his own reputation, and then played a key role in shaping the land that would become Saudi Arabia.

HUMBLE BEGINNINGS

The man who would one day boldly stand before the king and express his displeasure with British policies began his life under circumstances that offered no hint of his future success. Thomas Edward Lawrence was born on August 16, 1888, in Tremadoc, a town in northern Wales. It was only when he was a teenager that he would learn that his parents had never married, and that in fact his father was still married to another woman, with whom he had had several children before leaving them all for the family's governess.

The scandal remained hidden, in part because the family moved frequently. Lawrence was the third son in a family of five boys, all born in different countries. When the family finally settled in the university town of Oxford, England, Lawrence (known as Ned when he was a boy) was eight years old. His interest in history and architecture was fostered by bike trips to Welsh castles and throughout parts of France. By the time he had reached the age of 20, as a young Oxford university student, he decided to make a walking tour of the region of the world then known as the Ottoman Empire, passing through Syria, Palestine, and parts of Turkey. From July 9 until September 24, 1909, he explored cities like Beirut, Tripoli, and Nazareth, frequently battling sickness, often walking alone. By the time his journey had ended, he had covered nearly 1100 miles and begun a fascination with the Middle East that would mark his career. Returning to his university bearing gifts of various ancient treasures that he had found or purchased along the way, he also began to build his own reputation—of a fearless explorer and an expert on the Middle East.

Lawrence was awarded a special scholarship to perform research, and so by late December 1910 he set out from England to participate in archeological expeditions, digging up ruins in Egypt, in Palestine, and in Syria. For four years,

Pilgrimage to Mecca: View of Jiddah, c. 1900

The *hajj* is the pilgrimage to Mecca prescribed for every Muslim once in a lifetime—provided one can afford it and provided a person has enough provisions to leave for one's family during the absence.

The 1901 Appendix of *The Geographical Journal*, published by the Royal Geographical Society, acknowledges a photographic donation by G. P. Devey, Esq. and Sigr. L. Naretti of Massawa. The Curator noted: "Mr. Devey has already added many photographs to the Society's collection, and these which he has recently presented are specially welcome." The captions are handwritten on the original prints.

The first of the pictures of the pilgrimage is a photograph of the office of the camel-broker (*mukharrij*).

> As for the rental of camels and other mounts from Jidda to Mecca, this is in the charge of the camel broker (*mukharrij*) designated by the Sharif. [The Sharif is the guardian of the holy sites of Mecca and Medina.] All the camel-drivers must be listed on his records, and the pilgrims or their caravan leaders or the *wakils* who wish to rent camels must present themselves to the camel-broker and pay the rate fixed by the government . . . The camel driver receives his due from the broker.
>
> 1912 description quoted in F. E. Peters, *The Hajj* (1994)

Lawrence would assist several of the most noted archeologists of the time, including David Hogarth, Campbell Thompson, and Leonard Wooley. Lawrence made friends with some of the young Arabs working on the digs, and began to learn their language and customs. He was known for his ability to motivate these workers—a talent that would later serve him as he became involved in British efforts to establish connections with local Arab tribes.

For Lawrence, the Arab lands in which he worked transformed his life. Troubled by his undersized body and oversized intellect, life in England had been difficult for him. In the stark and serene beauty of the desert, he found a new world whose emptiness and simplicity appealed to him. The barren landscapes that he had excavated yielded up treasures, but, more importantly, they provided him with a sense of purpose. He took a genuine interest in the people whose history he was uncovering. He viewed them through many of the distortions of Western eyes (a sense of superiority, a need to educate them), but with one important difference: he valued their culture and did not want to see it "modernized" or transformed into some pale imitation of England.

By August 1914, Lawrence's archeological assignment had ended and he returned home to England. He was visiting his parents when it was announced that Britain had declared war on Germany. Both Britain and Germany had been competing for the strategic interests in the Middle East, and Lawrence's knowledge of the region, his experience in more remote areas, and his contacts among the Arab community made him a valuable source of information. As World War I began, Lawrence was assigned to a position with the British intelligence service and posted to the Middle East.

FALL OF AN EMPIRE

We have used the term "Middle East" to describe the region that was to make Lawrence famous, but at the time that he began his career in British intelligence this part of the world still formed part of the Ottoman Empire. The Ottomans were fierce warriors from the East who had built a mighty empire that was the most powerful in the world in the 1500s and 1600s. The empire was so vast that, at one point, it included significant portions of Asia, Europe, and northern Africa, as well as the countries we know today as Iran, Iraq, Syria, and Saudi Arabia. It was an Islamic empire, built on military conquests but tolerant of the different faiths of its far-flung subjects.

The success and growth the Ottoman Empire had experienced in medieval times was fading as the 19th century drew to a close. While attempts were made to modernize the empire, the sweeping changes brought about through science and technology enabled Western powers like Britain to build significant empires of their own. The Ottoman Empire found itself unable to adequately control the more remote regions of its territory, and slowly these began to slip away. Independence movements began to spring up in different regions, sparked in part by the corruption of the Ottoman ruler, known as the sultan. Upper-class citizens of the Ottoman Empire (the wealthy landowners, the religious and military leaders), enjoyed the benefits of close ties to the sultan, including a grant that prohibited them from paying taxes. The vast burden of paying for the luxurious lifestyle of the sultan and his family fell on those least able to pay—the peasants, farmers, and other members of the working class.

By the time that Lawrence began his first walking tour of parts of the Ottoman Empire, its glory was well behind it. An alliance had been formed between the Ottomans and Germany—many of the Ottoman military officers trained in German schools—but this alliance would drag them into a war that would bring a death sentence to the Ottoman Empire.

The territories of the Ottoman Empire were the site of fierce fighting during World War I. The Western powers, even before the war had ended, were busily making plans for how to carve up the Ottoman territories, should the war be decided in their favor. They knew that the Ottomans were weak and corrupt. They had no intention of letting

Pilgrimage to Mecca: El Haram, the holy place of Mecca, c. 1900

"Through the forest of columns [of the Haram] I could dimly see the great gravel-strewn quadrangle, over four and a half acres in extent; and in its midst, covered by a black cloth which made it hardly defined in the darkness, stood the Bayt Allah, the House of God, the Ka'ba.

Under the arches of the cloisters, bare-footed, long-robed, silent figures were hurrying to take up their positions behind the imams. In all parts of the great quadrangle, worshippers were forming into long lines facing the Ka'ba, preparing to perform the morning prayer. Over the crest of the hill of Abu Qubays, the first faint light of dawn showed in the sky, like a transparent patch in a sheet of dark-blue glass.

'Look,' said Abd al-Rahman, 'The Sacred House of God!'

I walked forward to the edge of the cloisters, and looked out across the wide court of the Mosque toward the great black-draped cube—that strange building, in the attempt to reach which tens of thousands, perhaps millions, of human beings have prematurely forfeited their lives; and seeing which, unnumbered millions have felt themselves to be on the very threshold of Paradise. It stood, with the simple massive grandeur of a solitary rock in the midst of the ocean—an expressive symbol of the Unity of that God Whose house it is. Aloof and mysterious it seemed, reared up majestically in the center of the great open quadrangle; while round and round its base the panting *Hajjis* hurried eagerly, uttering their pitiful supplication, 'O God, grant us, in the world, good; and, in the hereafter, good; and save us from the punishment of fire!'"

Eldon Rutter, *The Holy Cities of Arabia* (1930)

the fate of the region be decided by chance.

As early as 1914, foreign ministers from Britain and France had signed a treaty that spelled out their plans to carve up the parts of the Ottoman Empire that stretched across the Middle East. This treaty, later to be ratified by Russia as well, was known as the Sykes-Picot Treaty. It would cause a stir when its contents were finally revealed, making it clear that the Western powers had for years been making plans about how to shape the Middle East in a way they saw fit—a plan that, in most cases, ignored the thoughts or wishes of the people who lived there. Among those worried by this display of Western arrogance was the British intelligence officer who was helping to organize an Arab revolt that would greatly assist British plans—T.E. Lawrence.

ARAB REVOLT

By 1916, some British military efforts focused on splintering off the most vulnerable portions of the Ottoman Empire by establishing contact with tribal leaders in strategically important regions. In this way, military officials hoped to open up supply routes as well as to enlist the local tribes in fighting for Allied interests against the Ottoman forces. In these efforts, Lawrence's contacts and skills proved highly valuable. In October of 1916, he was sent out from Cairo to the region known as Arabia. A revolt was taking place—Arab armies had been formed and were fighting against the Ottoman forces, battling for their freedom and a land of their own.

This was a happy development indeed for the British, who did all they could to encourage the Arab revolt to help take Ottoman pressure off their own troops operating in the Sinai Desert. They had little intention of setting all of the Ottoman Empire free after the war's end, but this, of course, they did not reveal to the Arabs.

Instead, Lawrence was sent off to meet with representatives from the Arab armies, in part to determine who could best assist the British in their efforts to defeat Ottoman forces in the region. Lawrence's unwillingness to mince words made his reports useful, and occasionally entertaining, reading, as he dismissed one potential leader after another, listing an assortment of faults, from their excessive ambition to their inability to think and act independently.

Following a 100-mile journey under the heat of the Arabian sun on a camel, Lawrence at last found the leader he thought could best lead the Arab revolt (and so serve British interests). The Arabian *sheik* (a title of respect, often translated as "leader") Feisal al Hussain impressed Lawrence with his height and intelligence, with the way he commanded his men, and with his forceful opinions. Lawrence would soon join forces with Feisal, wearing Arab clothes and participating in the tribal revolt that would contribute to the war's end and the collapse of Ottoman strength in the region. He gained a reputation for bravery, a valuable asset amongst these fierce Arab tribes, and though wounded many times he continued to fight, leading a team of Arabs into the desert and engaging the Ottoman forces over and over again, freeing up British forces to invade Syria and Palestine.

In detailed letters to senior military officials, Lawrence described the incredible picture this Arab force made as it moved across the stark Arabian landscape: Feisal in front, dressed in sparkling white robes, with Lawrence on his left, clothed in bright red and white. Behind them flew three purple silk banners on long poles with gold spikes at the top. Next came three drummers playing a march, and behind them came 1200 camels, packed with supplies and bouncing close together, and a troop of men wearing brightly colored

Medina, c. 1880

This photograph of Medina ranks among the oldest still in existence. Notice the wall and the people in front of the image.

   This photograph was taken by Mohammed Sadic Bey, an eminent cartographer who had researched the tribes and roads of Arabia for decades. Sadic took his photographs while a colonel in the Egyptian army (with the honorific title of *Bey*).

clothing and all loudly singing a battle song praising Feisal and his family.

   It is not surprising that, by the time the war had ended, Lawrence had become famous. But he was also a man in conflict. He knew that he had betrayed the land and the men who had made him a celebrity. The Arabs under Feisal had fought fiercely for their independence—and the independence of all Arabs. But Britain had different plans. The territories of the Middle East were a valuable way to guarantee a direct route between Britain and its most treasured possession, India, and it was becoming increasingly clear that portions of the Ottoman Empire also possessed another asset: oil.

And so it was a conflicted Lawrence who was granted the honor of a meeting with his king, and a conflicted Lawrence who refused the military award offered to him. While his own future now looked bright and promising, the future of the land he had left behind seemed very uncertain.

Pilgrimage to Mecca: Rock near Mecca beneath which Muhammad would retire to meditate, c. 1900

2

The House of Saud

The history of the land we know today as Saudi Arabia is, in many ways, the history of one family—a family known by the name Al Saud. This family shaped a desert land governed by many different sheiks and rulers into a single country and then, with the discovery of oil beneath that desert sand, saw their country rise to the status of a world power.

Their story—the story of the creation of Saudi Arabia—began as the 19th century was drawing to an end, in the bleak desert sand of the southern part of Arabia, a land so forbidding that it was known as the Empty Quarter. Wandering through that desert landscape was a small tribe of refugees—the Saud family. They had once been one of the most powerful families in Arabia, including the holy cities of Mecca and Medina in their territory and dominating a vast stretch of land from Yemen to Syria, from the Red Sea to the Persian Gulf.

But this time of power lasted little more than 12 years. The Ottoman rulers in Constantinople were threatened by the family's holdings, and the twin holy cities were soon recaptured. The people fought fiercely against the Turkish army, but ultimately the leader of the Saud family was forced to surrender. He was transported to Constantinople, where his head was cut off and his headless body displayed as a warning to any other rebellious citizens.

The Saud family left behind the shattered remains of their palaces and relocated, this time to Riyadh. Here, their dreams were smaller, and for nearly a century they ruled over a narrower stretch of land. But this territory, too, would soon be snatched away, in yet another series of bloody battles, this time with the Rashid tribe.

The Saud family, seeking shelter in the inhospitable sands of the Empty Quarter, seemed to have been defeated. Living in tents made of black goat hair, traveling on camels, they moved south in the heat of the summer, seeking water. Theirs was a nomadic life. And growing up in this difficult climate was a young teenager named Abdul Aziz Ibn Saud.

Abdul Aziz studied the ways of the Bedouins, the nomads with whom he lived. Lacking a permanent home, sleeping at night in the open, he had no luxuries. His blanket was made of rough wool from camel's hair. The camels the tribe rode and used were their most prized possessions. The stories Abdul Aziz learned growing up seemed like fairy tales—tales of a time when his family had once been one of the most powerful in all of Arabia.

But as Abdul Aziz grew older, he became firmly convinced that his life had a single purpose: to avenge his family's honor, to recapture the land they had once held, and to restore the Saud family to the highest position in Arabia.

Pilgrimage to Mecca: Attending the prayer around the Ka'ba, c. 1900

For a while, these hopes seemed merely the dreams of a restless teenager. For two years, Abdul Aziz lived in the desert with his family, absorbing the lessons of the bedouins with whom the family traveled. He learned self-confidence—the kind of self-confidence that comes of carving a living out of the harshest conditions, of going without any luxuries, of sleeping in the open. He learned the importance of the unit, rather than the individual, as the bedouin caravans transported men, women, and children, plus all their necessary supplies, on camels for long distances through the desert.

The family soon moved to the port of Kuwait, where they stayed for several years. It was a humble existence in a house made of mud with only three rooms in a damp and smelly back alley. Abdul Aziz was a good Muslim, and following the tradition of the time he married early, at the age of 16. The cramped family quarters damaged the health of Abdul's young wife, though, and only six months after their marriage she died.

In later years, Abdul would not look back with fondness on the six years he lived in Kuwait, but it was while the family struggled to survive in the port city that the Saud family's dream of recapturing some of their past glory began to seem possible. For the ruler of Kuwait at that time was a sheik named Mubarak Al Sabah, and he was always looking for ways to strengthen Kuwait—and his position as ruler in the process. Today, we think of Kuwait as one of the richest territories in the globe, significant because of its vast resources of oil. But at the time Abdul Aziz and his family lived there, Kuwait was viewed as little more than a port— a port through which goods from the outside world passed into central Arabia.

Sheik Mubarak decided that the surest way to keep Kuwait significant was to make sure that Arabia was weaker. And the fastest way to a weak Arabia was to divide it. Sheik Mubarak felt that the Rashid family was too confident in its control of central Arabia. It was time to test their power—and to make sure that the Rashid family did not entertain any thoughts of invading Kuwait. A diversion was called for, and he decided that the perfect diversion would be a new attack on Riyadh by the Saud family.

Sheik Mubarak began to meet with Abdul Aziz, and to help him shape a more realistic plan out of his dreams of restoring his family to honor and glory. And as Abdul spent more and more time with his mentor, a plot was slowly hatched that would lead him back to Arabia and turn the Saud family's dreams of a return to power into a reality.

THE BATTLE BEGINS

In the early part of 1901, Sheik Mubarak decided to test the waters by launching an attack on the Rashid forces. He had directed an army of bedouins, with members of the Saud family in their midst, to attack a section of Rashid territory around Ha'il. Their forces were soundly defeated, and in response the Al Rashid launched their own attack on Mubarak's Kuwaiti territory.

But as news of the Rashid plans to conquer Kuwait reached British ears, there was great alarm. Sheik Mubarak had been willing to allow British ships access to the Kuwaiti port. The Al Rashid might prove friendlier to German interests. So British ships quickly steamed into the Kuwaiti harbor, and British forces joined up with the Mubarak army to turn back the invaders.

Kuwait was safe. And suddenly Abdul Aziz recognized that the time had come to launch his own attack. The Rashid forces, dismayed at their unexpected defeat, were far from Riyadh, still focusing on the challenge Mubarak had presented. Their distractedness offered a chance for a surprise attack, and Abdul Aziz was determined to seize it.

He was only 21 years old, but he had been planning this moment for a long time. He gathered together a party of about 40 men, including his half-brother Muhammad and several of his cousins. They were determined to recapture

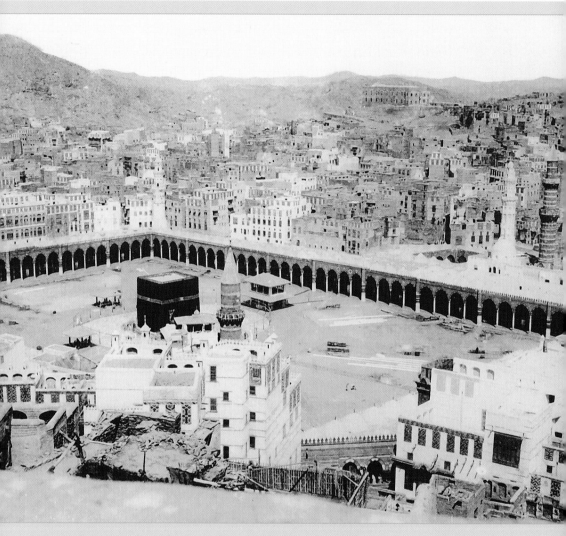

Pilgrimage to Mecca: Another view of the Ka'ba, c. 1900

Riyadh and avenge their family honor, or die in the attempt.

The party rode south and west on camels in September 1901, trying to drum up support for the attack as they traveled. Gradually, their numbers grew, until some 200 men were preparing to attack Riyadh from the south. But as Abdul Aziz made plans to launch his attack, his initial hopes of a quick success began to fade. He learned that his plans for a surprise attack had somehow been leaked to the Al Rashid, who had busily set about fortifying the city. The weather had turned, growing cold at night and making sleeping out in the desert a difficult and uncomfortable prospect. Abdul Aziz's warrior party, promised a quick fight and sudden riches, became less enthusiastic at the prospect of a prolonged attack and few provisions to supply them until the battles were over. Gradually, his fighting force began to slip away, until Abdul Aziz found himself in charge of no more than 60 or 70 men.

Abdul Aziz gathered his small force together and explained the dangers they faced. He had no intention of returning in defeat to Kuwait, but he offered his men the chance to return home. Instead, they chose to fight with him—to the death.

With this small band of faithful men, Abdul Aziz plotted the only strategy that gave them a chance. They retreated away from Riyadh, heading south. And there, they disappeared. To the Rashid soldiers stationed at Riyadh, it seemed as if the Al Saud army had given up and headed back to Kuwait.

For 50 days, Abdul Aziz and his men hid in the desert of the Empty Quarter—the very desert where he had first learned the ways of the Bedouins. He used his lessons well. During those long days, he and his men rested. At night, under cover of darkness, they crept out of their hiding places to drink and eat the little they could find. Then, brushing the sand to sweep away any traces of their footsteps, they slipped back into hiding.

Finally, on the night of January 15, 1902, the time had come for them to make their desperate attempt to win back the Saud family's honor. As darkness spread over the city of Riyadh, Abdul Aziz and his men walked quietly out of the desert. Carrying the few weapons they had—some swords and daggers, a rifle or two—they slipped up to the unsuspecting guards patrolling the city's walls. A small scouting party of about six men, including Abdul Aziz, climbed up quickly over the wall and headed for the garrison where the Rashidi army kept its supplies and weapons.

Their first stop was the governor's house, just across from the garrison. They tied up the governor's wife, and then one man crept back to the troop to bring reinforcements. They gathered quietly, waiting for the sun to rise, when the governor would emerge from his base at the garrison and head back across the street for home and breakfast. Finally, after several hours, they saw the governor appear and move across the street to his home.

Abdul Aziz wasted no time. He charged forward at the governor, who immediately attempted to rush back into the protective walls of the garrison. But the governor was too late. Abdul Aziz tackled him, and the rest of the Al Saud forces swiftly joined him, fighting off the governor's guards, who were attempting to pull the governor back into the garrison. But Abdul Aziz held him tight. This tug-of-war went on for several seconds, until the governor managed to free himself and was pulled inside.

The quick thinking of one of Abdul Aziz's cousins saved the day. He threw himself into the garrison and managed to get off a shot that killed the governor. In a matter of minutes, the battle was over. Abdul Aziz's forces had triumphed. The garrison surrendered, and Abdul Aziz was in charge of Riyadh. The Saud family once more controlled the very heart of Arabia.

THE BEGINNING OF A KINGDOM

The Rashid family had ruled Riyadh and the surrounding territories with fierce and tyrannical methods, methods that had proved effective while they were in power but quickly were used against them the minute a portion of their territory began to slip away. The Bedouins who lived in the deserts surrounding Riyadh were delighted to learn of the defeat of the Al Rashid. They quickly traveled to Riyadh to see the young victor whose father had once ruled them, and to promise their loyalty.

Their pledges to serve Abdul Aziz were valuable. Arabia at the time was ruled by a fierce assembly of different sheiks whose territories were not reflected by clear lines on a map, but instead by the number of bedouin nomads who agreed to support them. Abdul Aziz had captured Riyadh, but the land beyond that—the full extent of the territory retaken by the Saud family—depended largely on which of the bedouin tribes agreed to accept him as their *emir*, or leader.

The extent of the land controlled by Abdul Aziz was still to be determined, but one thing was certain—this new kingdom was surrounded by enemies. The Al Rashid had been driven back up to the north, but they would certainly reassemble there and attempt to retake Riyadh. The east, containing the valuable access to the Persian Gulf, was controlled by Turkish forces from the Ottoman Empire. In the west, where the holy cities of Mecca and Medina were found, was a vast stretch of land known as the Hejaz, controlled by the Sharif of Mecca. This was the greatest prize of all Arabia, for the Hejaz was of both religious and financial significance. For faithful Muslims, the pilgrimage to Mecca is one of the most important tenets of their religion. At least once in his life, a devout Muslim—if he is physically and financially able—is expected to attempt to travel to Mecca, and the annual rites surrounding this pilgrimage, with the arrival of tens of thousands of faithful Muslims, meant that Mecca was a very wealthy city indeed. Mecca was a gathering place—a city where Muslims from many different countries came together not only to worship, but to trade goods and share ideas.

Pilgrimage to Mecca: West side of Mina Valley, c. 1900

"On arriving at Wadi Mina, each nation encamped upon the spot which custom has assigned to it at every returning *Hajj*. After disposing of the baggage, the *Hajjis* hastened to the ceremony of throwing stones at the devil. It is said that when Abraham returned from the pilgrimage to Arafat and arrived at the Wadi Mina, the devil Iblis presented himself before him at the entrance of the valley, to obstruct passage; then the Angel Gabriel, who accompanied the Patriarch, advised him to throw stones at him, which he did, and after pelting him seven times, Iblis retired. When Abraham reached the middle of the valley, he again appeared before him, and for the last time, at its western extremity, and was both times repulsed by the same number of stones . . . "

John Burckhardt, *Travels in Arabia* (1829)

As Abdul Aziz examined the land once more captured by the Saud family, one thing became clear. He had only one ally: the northeastern port of Kuwait. He needed more allies if he was to hold on to Riyadh, and he needed them quickly.

As Bedouin leaders continued to arrive to pledge their loyalty, Abdul Aziz ordered his forces to repair the city's walls in preparation for an attack. He sent for his family, and the arrival of his father was greeted with enthusiastic cheers. But there was little debate about who the new leader of the Saud family would be. Abdul Aziz's father publicly declared that he was stepping down in favor of his son, presenting him with a magnificent sword as a symbol of the handing over of power from one generation to the next.

Abdul Aziz wasted little time basking in the praise of the people of Riyadh, or the admiration of the bedouins. He knew that he must quickly assemble a stronger army, to defend the city from those who would seek to take it back. He soon rode back into the desert, heading south in search of fighters to join his side.

Abdul Aziz was young, but he was an impressive physical presence—standing nearly 6'3", much taller than many of the other Bedouins. He had the noble heritage of the Saud family, and the glory of his recent success in Riyadh. But that was about all. He needed something to attract a new breed of warriors to his cause. He could not offer them money—his family had almost none. But he believed that his cause was just and right and that it was a holy quest. And it was through this conviction that he found the source for his new army.

A NEW CRUSADE

In the desert surrounding Riyadh lived a group who practiced a particularly strict form of Islam. They did not drink or smoke; they shunned fine foods and fine clothes, believing that most worldly comforts and pleasures were sinful. They were known as Wahhabis, named after the man (Muhammad bin Abd al-Wahhab) who had proclaimed their strict interpretation of the Koran in the 18th century. Wahhab had been sheltered by the Saud family in the mid-1700s, and the relationship had benefited both sides. Wahhab had preached a philosophy of reform and conversion—that it was the duty of good Muslims not merely to shape their own lives to follow the dictates of the Koran, but also to ensure that their neighbors did as well. Wahhabis believed that loyalty to Islam should exceed tribal loyalty—Muslims, they felt, were part of a worldwide community of believers, not simply an isolated tribe of faithful worshippers. For the Wahhabis, Muslims who did not share their views were no better than unbelievers—they were enemies of God. If preaching and sharing their experiences was not enough, then conversion would need to be done by force. This sense of engaging in a kind of holy war became the motivation for the Saud family to move out from their base into other parts of Arabia in the 18th century. By the beginning of the 19th century, the Al Saud, united and inspired by Wahhabi teaching, had taken control of Mecca and Medina and ruled over a vast empire.

While the Saudi empire did not last into the 20th century, the links between the Al Saud and the Wahhabis had not been forgotten. As Abdul Aziz began to plan a way to reinforce his army, it did not take him long to remember the fiercely determined Wahhabis. He decided that it was time for him to get married again—and the bride he chose was the daughter of Riyadh's leading religious authority, the chief of the spiritual leaders known as the *ulema*. He also happened to be a direct descendent of Muhammad ibn Abdul Wahhab.

For seven months, Abdul Aziz built up an army, courting the ulema by granting them the authority to set all laws in Riyadh and oversee all questions of morality. He rode out into the desert, meeting with Bedouin leaders, eating and

Pilgrimage to Mecca: Pilgrim's arrival at Mount Arafat, c. 1900

According to Islam, Adam and Eve recognized each other on this hill after wandering for a hundred years apart.

praying with them, even sleeping outdoors with them before setting off for the next Bedouin tribe. He needed as much support as he could muster, for word had reached him that the Rashid family was on the move, planning to retake the land they had lost.

The battle came not in Riyadh, with its newly fortified walls, but in a small settlement south of the city. There Abdul Aziz had stationed his men among the palm trees, ordering them to lay still and silent, hiding behind their camel saddles. There they watched and waited for the Rashidi forces to move into the open.

It seems a straightforward approach to battle, but to the bedouins it represented a revolutionary idea. The Rashid forces had never encountered an enemy that fought from fixed positions. They were unsuspecting as they rode forward into the open, only to be immediately fired upon from various spots in the palm groves. The bursts of rifle fire continued all day, and ultimately the Rashid forces were forced to retreat.

The next day, Abdul Aziz's men once more resumed their position, but to their surprise they saw the Rashid forces packing up and moving out. There would be no second day of fighting. And for the Al Saud forces, it was just as well. For what the Rashid army did not realize was that the solid day of rifle fire had used up nearly every last bit of ammunition Abdul Aziz's troops had. They would not have managed another day of fighting. But the Rashid army had given up, and once more Abdul Aziz's forces had triumphed.

As news of his two victories traveled from settlement to settlement, Abdul Aziz soon found his territory expanding as more tribal leaders arrived to pledge their loyalty. Only a year and a half after he had first launched his attack on Riyadh, he was in control of a region that stretched a hundred miles to the north and a hundred miles to the south of the city that would become the capital of his new kingdom.

A KINGDOM RESTORED

By the spring of 1904, the Rashid family had begun to realize that the threat posed by Abdul Aziz and the Saudi army might be much greater than they had originally imagined. Now that the Saudis had successfully won back

Pilgrimage to Mecca: The Prophet's Tomb ("The Garden of Purity"), c. 1900

Medina is celebrated as the place from which Muhammad conquered all of Arabia after his flight from Mecca (622 A.D.), and a pilgrimage is made to his tomb in the city's chief mosque. As with Mecca, only Muslims are allowed to enter the city.

Abdulmecid I, Sultan of the Ottoman Empire (1839–61), initiated a project for the virtual reconstruction of the mosque in 1848 and completed it in 1860. This was the last renovation of the mosque before its current expansion completed between 1953 and 1955.

so much of their old territory, it was only a matter of time before they began to think about conquering the land traditionally held by the Al Rashid, as well. The Al Rashid turned to the powerful Ottoman army for assistance. Abdul

Aziz wasted little time turning to his own superpower. He sent his own request for help and supplies, directed to the representative of the British Empire in the Persian Gulf, a man named Percy Cox.

Cox was noteworthy for his genuine admiration for the Arabs and his interest in the political situation in Arabia. He could speak Arabic, and had built a reputation as a British representative who could be trusted. He also had built a friendship with Abdul Aziz's old friend and mentor from Kuwait, Sheik Mubarak. The British had proved a useful ally to Mubarak, sending in warships to the Kuwaiti ports just as the Ottoman Turks seemed poised to attack. Perhaps they would be willing to provide the same defensive support to the Saud family.

Percy Cox was inclined to assist the Saud family, but other British politicians were divided among those who supported the Rashid faction, those who believed that British interests in Arabia went no further than the coastland, and those who supported the Al Saud. For several months, these competing factions exchanged letters and telegrams debating their respective opinions. And while the correspondence flew back and forth between various British offices, Abdul Aziz ran out of time. In early 1904 the Ottoman forces joined up with the army of the Rashid faction, and by summer Abdul Aziz's forces were assembled in the desert east of Anayzah, only a short distance from their enemies.

The Ottoman Turks had brought an advantage to the Rashid side: artillery. Abdul Aziz's fighters were fierce bedouin warriors but they had never encountered artillery fire, and so the first battle quickly forced the Saudi army into retreat, with their leader wounded in his hand and leg. The only thing that saved them from complete defeat was a slim advantage—they were used to fighting in the desert heat. The Turkish forces were not. And as the heat of summer beat down on the two camps, the Turkish soldiers, unaccustomed to the desert and having marched hundreds of miles to reach the site of the battle, were suffering.

After that initial battle, the two sides essentially faced each other in a kind of stalemate. For several weeks, neither moved—there were few places in the area to fight over, and both armies were battling cholera and an increasing desire for the battle to be over. In the end, it was the Rashid forces that blinked first. Their fighters finally had enough, and decided that they would leave for home. The Saudi army caught them as they attempted to sneak away one night, and they were quickly overwhelmed. Their Turkish allies were also soon overpowered.

While the victory was significant, even more important was what was captured—the Turkish artillery. But Abdul Aziz understood that the vast Ottoman Empire had many more forces to dispatch into the desert, and he had no wish to take his chances again against a force vastly superior in numbers to his own. He decided that the time had come for diplomacy, so he sent his father to serve as his representative to the Ottomans. The negotiations were ultimately successful, and by 1905 the Turkish authorities had agreed to recognize the Saud family's rightful possession of the territory they currently held. In exchange, Abdul Aziz agreed to serve as the Ottoman district commissioner for the territory, in effect agreeing to submit to Ottoman policies in his land.

It was not an arrangement that would last long. By the spring of 1906, the forces of Abdul Aziz once again fought the Rashid army, and once more defeated them, this time killing the leader of the family. Chaos ensued among the Al Rashid, as various relatives competed to be named the new leader of the tribe. With northern Arabia caught up in intrigue and chaos, Abdul Aziz had little to fear from the Rashid forces. And so the need for his Turkish alliance

Pilgrimage to Mecca: The tomb of Khadija and other monuments, c. 1900

The following description was written in 1925, after the Wahhabis under Ibn Saud had gained power in this area. The Wahhabi is a member of the Muslim "puritan" movement founded by Muhammad ibn 'Abd al-Wahhab in the 18th century and adopted by the Saud family in 1744. The Wahhabis deny all acts implying polytheism, such as visiting tombs and venerating saints. They advocate a return to the original teachings of Islam.

"The Famous cemetery of Ma'ala occupies twenty or thirty acres of ground at the northern end of the Meccan Valley ... Here, according to tradition, are buried the Prophet's mother, Amina; his wife, Khadija, and his ancestors Abd Manaf and Abd al-Muttalib, together with a number of famous early Muslims. The *mutawwifs* [the official guides] have invented long supplications and pious exercises to be said at these tombs. The tolerant men among the Wahhabis term these exercises 'undesirable innovation,' while the many intolerant Wahhabis call them rites of polytheism ... The tombs of these personages were formerly crowned with small but handsome domes [see above photograph], but these, without exception, have been demolished, together with most of the tombstones."

Eldon Rutter, *The Holy Cities of Arabia* (1930)

Rutter, an English convert to Islam, was performing his first *Hajj*. And, the *Hajj* of 1925 was the first under the political auspices of the House of Saud and the first in more than a century to reflect the religious teachings of the followers of 'Abd al-Wahhab. Therefore, Rutter had an unparalleled opportunity to observe the old order yield to the new.

began to fade. His tribes were soon raiding Turkish supply caravans, and before long the Ottoman army, crippled by defectors and political problems back in Constantinople, began to pull out of central Arabia.

In only a few years, Abdul Aziz was firmly in control of a large stretch of Arabian territory. Having successfully defeated the Rashid forces in the north, and having outlasted the Ottoman forces, he began to turn his gaze to the west. The holy cities of Mecca and Medina had once been part of the Saudi empire. As a devout Muslim, Abdul Aziz felt a divine call to see them once more come under the protection of the Saud family.

Ibn Saud's standards on the move, March 8, 1911

This and all other pictures in this chapter were photographed by Captain William Henry I. Shakespear.

3

King of Arabia

n the spring of 1910, Abdul Aziz was 35 years old. He arrived in Kuwait to visit his old friend Sheik Mubarak. By now, the British fully understood how powerful Abdul Aziz was becoming, and the British political representative in Kuwait, a man named Captain William Shakespear (a distant descendant of the famous writer), decided to invite him to dinner. Captain Shakespear was impressed by Abdul Aziz's openness and amazed by his generosity.

It was during a second meeting that Abdul Aziz explained his plans. He had determined to recapture from the hated Ottomans the province of al Hasa, which lay along the eastern coast of the Persian Gulf. The Ottomans had seized that land in 1871; Abdul

Aziz had decided that the time had come to take it back.

If he had expected the British representative to offer his support or encouragement, he was disappointed. Captain Shakespear quickly explained that Britain had a good relationship with the Ottoman Empire and had no wish to participate in an attack against it. At a meeting two months later, the subject once more arose. By now, the Ottoman Empire was crumbling, and its armies were being pulled back closer and closer to home to hold onto the remaining bits of territory. Other Ottoman subjects were gaining their independence; Abdul Aziz was determined that Arabia would join this group.

Captain Shakespear once more cautioned Abdul Aziz against any attack, explaining that Britain would not be able to support his efforts. He then sent off a report of the meeting to his superiors, convinced by Abdul Aziz's disappointment that he understood that an attack would be disastrous. But on the same day that he sent off his report, he learned that Saudi troops had invaded al Hasa. The region had fallen, and a significant portion of the Persian Gulf coast now belonged to Abdul Aziz. It would one day prove to be some of the most valuable land on earth.

Britain would soon have cause to reassess the somewhat dismissive attitude it had initially adopted to offers of alliance from Abdul Aziz. Only five months after he had successfully seized al Hasa, Britain found itself on the opposite side from the Ottoman Empire as World War I began. Suddenly, the geography of Arabia took on a new strategic importance, as both sides quickly attempted to cement their positions to ensure safe passage of their ships and supplies. When it became clear that the Rashid forces had united with the Ottomans, Britain suddenly became very interested in the plans of Abdul Aziz.

Captain Shakespear was drafted into service once more, this time to try to persuade Abdul Aziz to agree to an alliance quite similar to the one he himself had proposed several months earlier. But Abdul Aziz, having been turned down twice before, was no longer so eager to attach himself to the British. As Shakespear attempted to plead the British cause, Abdul Aziz's attention was focused elsewhere—on an imminent battle with the Rashid forces north of Riyadh. Abdul Aziz suggested to Shakespear that he leave the camp quickly, as the pending battle was certain to be bloody and fierce. But Shakespear knew that the battle would have strategic significance for the larger war being fought. If the Rashid army—linked with the Ottomans—should lose, Britain would be in a much stronger position in the Middle East. It was an opportunity to witness a potentially historic battle, and Shakespear decided to remain.

But the victory Shakespear had hoped to witness did not happen. Instead, the Saudi forces were quickly overpowered and fled. Shakespear was shot and died on the battlefield, and with this single battle Abdul Aziz determined that his Saudi forces would play no role in the unfolding conflict that would become World War I.

The battle marked another critical turning point, as well. Shakespear had pleaded the cause of Abdul Aziz to his superiors, and they had considered the possibility of an alliance with the Saudi leader as a way to cement British ties to the Arab world. But after Shakespear's death, another Englishman, also skilled at forming relationships with the Bedouins, would have tremendous influence on the course of Britain's opinion of the Arabs. His name was T.E. Lawrence, and he had a very different candidate in mind to be the leader of the Arab revolt: the third son of the Sharif of Mecca, Feisal al Hussain.

Bedouin women at al-Himua Wells, near Thaj, March 5, 1911

William Henry I. Shakespear (1878-1915) was an explorer of eastern and central Arabia. Shakespear, the son of a British colonial officer in the Indian Forest Service, was born in India in 1878. He trained with the Indian regiment, the Bengal Lancers, before transferring to the British consular service. He served in Persia and eastern Arabia, later becoming British political agent in Kuwait. Known as Captain Shakespear, he made six exploratory expeditions in eastern Arabia, and in 1914, crossed the Arabian Peninsula from Kuwait via Riyadh to Sinai, traveling across more than 1,200 miles of unmapped country.

As political agent in Kuwait, Shakespear became convinced that Ibn Saud (1880–1953) was the only Arab leader capable of bringing together the disparate tribes of the desert in an alliance with Great Britain against the Ottoman Empire. Despite a series of detailed reports, the Foreign Office remained unconvinced. "The objections to a policy of adventure," London replied, had not diminished. Instead, Shakespear was instructed to confine his travels to the immediate surroundings of Kuwait and do nothing to allow Ibn Saud to think that Great Britain regarded him as anything more than just another Arabian tribal chief. However, in November 1914, Great Britain and the Ottoman Empire were at war. Shakespear now was asked to negotiate with Ibn Saud and "to ensure at all costs" that Ibn Saud was kept out of the Turkish camp. On January 24, 1915, at age thirty-six, Shakespear was killed fighting alongside Ibn Saud against Ibn Rashid, Saud's pro-Turkish enemy. In time, Shakespear's evaluation that Ibn Saud would become one of the world's most powerful rulers proved correct. And, years after Shakespear was long dead, Ibn Saud was asked to name the greatest of the Europeans he had met in his life. He replied unhesitatingly: "Captain Shakespear!"

The illustrations were selected from Shakespear's photographic scrapbooks, which have been deposited with the Royal Geographical Society. These scrapbooks are the only photographic record of the rise of the House of Saud and the foundations of Saudi Arabia.

A WEAKENED EMPIRE

It seems tempting, with the wisdom of hindsight, to argue that Britain should have devoted more support to Abdul Aziz, rather than to Feisal al Hussain. But as World War I unfolded, Abdul Aziz was busy with his own problems, and in no position to assist the British in their efforts to spark an Arab revolt against the Ottoman Empire. A group of rebellious sheiks were attempting to wrest parts of their land away from the Saudi empire. They had no interest in paying taxes to support the Saudi family in distant Riyadh, and they eventually forced a series of disastrous battles. At the time that Lawrence of Arabia was creating his own legend, assisting Feisal's forces in over-powering the vastly superior Ottoman armies, Abdul Aziz was fighting simply to hold on to what he had.

It was a subdued Abdul Aziz who finally agreed to meet with Percy Cox in December 1915 to conclude the discussions that had been begun by Captain Shakespear. Both sides left the meeting satisfied with their new Anglo-Saudi friendship treaty. Britain was granted trading privileges and oversight of the Saudi foreign policy. Abdul Aziz received a guarantee of British protection against Saudi enemies and much-needed weapons and cash. Within a year, the influx of supplies and money enabled Abdul Aziz to firmly stamp out any rebellions and begin the process of setting up an independent Saudi state in central Arabia.

With central Arabia firmly in his hands, Abdul Aziz was becoming a valuable ally for the British, but the flouting of power by another British ally—the Sharif of Mecca—was beginning to annoy him. Sharif Hussain had gone so far as to declare himself the "king of all Arabs," but Abdul Aziz had little intention of sharing his empire with anyone.

THE MAN WHO WOULD BE KING

Sharif Hussain had been lobbying for British support to ensure the continuance of his kingdom in Arabia for several years, but prior to that his power had depended on the support and favor of the Ottoman Empire. It was due to the rulers of the empire in Istanbul that he had been granted the right to rule over Mecca and Medina, as well as the region of Arabia known as the Hejaz. His family claimed to be descended from the prophet Muhammad, but it was his relationship with the Ottomans, more than his family lineage, that had placed him in charge of this prized part of Arab territory.

As we have seen from the story of Lawrence of Arabia, British powers spent much of the time before and after World War I carving up the Middle East and choosing rulers for the region who would ultimately be favorable to British interests. As they studied the competing rivals—Abdul Aziz and Sharif Hussain—they understood that they were choosing between the two opposite sides of Arabia. Both men had family ties that had linked them to Arabian soil for generations. Both men were eager to build an alliance with the British to ensure their continued political standing. And both men hoped to ultimately rule over all of Arabia. But that was essentially where the similarities began and ended.

Sharif Hussain was approximately 20 years older than Abdul Aziz, and he was no desert Bedouin. He was a city dweller, and the heart of his kingdom was in the bustling urban centers of Mecca, Medina, and Jiddah. Unlike Abdul Aziz, whose kingdom was in need of cash, Sharif Hussain ruled over a territory whose economy was thriving, largely based on the annual influx of Muslim pilgrims coming to Mecca. Much of Mecca's economy was based on providing supplies and shelter to the pilgrims, generally at largely inflated prices. The luxuries available in Mecca were abhorrent to Abdul Aziz's Wahhabi supporters, who viewed what had happened to the unofficial capital of the Muslim faith as symbolic of the need for a complete reform of Islam.

The two men were as different in temperament and personality as the territories over which they ruled. Both were clever men, but whereas Abdul Aziz was known for being frank and outspoken, Sharif Hussain delighted in puzzling the British who courted him, and many frustrated diplomats would leave his presence uncertain whether their meeting had been a success or failure.

The British ultimately chose to back Sharif Hussain, although competing forces within the British administration quarreled bitterly over the choice. But there were several valid arguments for supporting the Sharif of Mecca over the ruler of central Arabia.

First was the simple fact of geography. Central Arabia was difficult to travel, and largely unfamiliar territory to the majority of British administrators in the region. The advantage Sharif Hussain's kingdom offered—access to the Red Sea—provided strategic value. His title—Sharif of Mecca—underscored the fact that he was in control of what many Arabs viewed as the most important city of all. His position as guardian of the holy city meant that he could offer potential leadership not only to the Muslims of Arabia, but to Muslims throughout the world.

Britain's goal was to spark an Arab revolt against the Ottomans. They hoped for this to stretch across all of the former Ottoman territories—most critically, Arabia, Syria, and Palestine, as well as Turkey. Sharif Hussain's family ties stretched beyond Mecca and Medina to include connections in Turkey, Syria, and Palestine. All of this made him the logical candidate for Britain to back, and so they did.

Watering at al-Himua Wells, near Thaj, March 5, 1911

It was a bitter disappointment to Abdul Aziz. But he did not abandon his dreams of a united Arabia under Saudi leadership. Instead, he turned elsewhere for assistance, to a small settlement some 160 miles from Riyadh, a settlement peopled by a group of religious zealots known as the *Ikhwan* (the Brotherhood).

The Ikhwan were linked to the Wahhabis in that they devoutly believed in living their life in complete accordance with the teachings of the Koran and the Hadith (the collection of sayings and doings of Muhammad). Abdul Aziz had supported the Ikhwan, giving them land, supplies, and even encouraging new missionaries to join with the Ikhwan's crusade to convert the Bedouins.

It was an investment that would prove very wise indeed, for as World War I began to wind down, Abdul Aziz knew that the supplies Britain had given to Sharif Hussain to overthrow the Ottomans might soon be turned against Riyadh. The Sharif had not proclaimed himself "king of all Arabs" for nothing, and Abdul Aziz knew that the Saudi territory was one of the few remaining obstacles in Sharif Hussain's effort to claim the entire peninsula as his own.

A basic tenet of the Ikhwan philosophy was that most modern ways merely served to get in the way of true faith. Singing and dancing were banned; most children's games were banned; smoking, radios and telephones were banned; even gold, silk, and jewelry were considered out of step with the teachings of Muhammad.

In this austere setting, Abdul Aziz saw opportunity. Many of the Ikhwan were Bedouins, used to life in the desert and the practice of raiding other camps for supplies. These were no urban priests, preaching a message of faith in comfortable settings and urging their followers to abstain from the temptations surrounding them. These were raiders, who believed that anyone killed in a holy war would go immediately to Paradise, for their death had been for a just and noble cause. They did not seek converts only through example—they also sought them by force. And they were well-armed for their cause.

By 1917, the Ikhwan had spread out through the Nadj region of central Arabia. There were over 200 of their settlements, and within those settlements, some 60,000 men of fighting age were ready to go into battle—provided that it was for a holy cause. Abdul Aziz had an entire army at his disposal—he only needed to determine how and when to use it.

He did not have long to wait. Within a year, World

War I was ending. Sharif Hussain, confident of British support, had determined that the time had come to cement his hold over all of Arabia. He sent a force, headed up by his son Abdullah, to subdue the regions that lay between Mecca and Riyadh, a territory known as Kurmah, in part because those lands had recently become the targets of Ikhwan missionaries. It quickly became clear that Abdullah had no intention of stopping once he had taken Kurmah; instead, he planned to continue on to seize Riyadh and proceed until he had scooped up all of the Saudi territory.

Abdullah had not reckoned on the Ikhwan. Stories of the brave fighting of the Ikhwan missionaries in Kurmah, struggling against Abdullah's forces, had sparked the fury of the Ikhwan. Their fellow believers were in danger—a clear call for holy war.

The Ikhwan could travel for hundreds of miles with only the most minimal supplies. They were fierce fighters, who believed that they were on a mission from God. They moved swiftly across the desert, a huge army riding on camels. They found Abdullah's forces asleep, and immediately began killing every man they could find. For them, death was the ultimate goal, and so they were completely fearless in battle. By the time the sun rose, only a handful of men (including Abdullah) had escaped.

The Ikhwan were ready to move on to Mecca, which would have been essentially defenseless without Abdullah's forces to block their advance. But Abdul Aziz did not want to conquer Mecca. He saw the holy city as a piece of a much larger empire, one that needed to be built on rightful leadership as much as on conquest. So the Ikhwan returned to their settlements and Abdul Aziz continued to wait for the right time to claim a much larger kingdom.

Ibn Saud Abdul Aziz with brothers and sons, March 11, 1911

END OF THE RASHIDS

It was not easy to subdue the Ikhwan, once they had been called to battle. But it was not long before once more Abdul Aziz summoned his troops. By 1920, the Rashid family's own internal struggle for power had reached a deadly climax, with the ruler shot dead by his cousin and the cousin then quickly executed. It had been a deadly kingdom to try to control, with one after another of the heirs killed either in battle with the Saudis or by members of their own family. The sole survivor of this deadly tussle was a young boy of 18 whose mother was a slave.

Abdul Aziz knew that the weakened kingdom could not face a serious challenge, and that its people might be looking for a more inspiring ruler than the son of a slave. And he was correct. Within three weeks, the war between the Rashid forces and the Saudis—a war that had lasted, on and off, for 20 years—was over. The kingdom belonged to Abdul Aziz.

Abdul Aziz had triumphed once more. But a whole new set of problems were presenting themselves to the newly proclaimed Sultan, to be known as Ibn Saud (son of Saud), and at the heart of them lay the British.

In a meeting in Cairo, held in March of 1921, the British Secretary of State for the Colonies, a man named Winston Churchill, decided that the time had come to resolve the status of the Middle East once and for all. He gathered together a collection of experts—which included T.E. Lawrence—and gave them the task of deciding how best to carve up the Middle East.

It was an astounding bit of Western arrogance. The conference of "Middle Eastern experts" consisted of 35 Englishmen (and one woman—Gertrude Bell) and only two Arabs (both aides to Sharif Hussain's son Feisal). It is perhaps not surprising that the conference determined that the former pieces of the Ottoman Empire could best be governed by Western nations and/or leaders they had specifically selected. In short order, the Middle East was divided: Palestine to the British, Syria and Lebanon to the French. Even more disturbing to Abdul Aziz was the dividing up of the remaining land among members of Sharif Hussain's family. The Sharif himself was proclaimed the King of the Hejaz. His son, Feisal, was proclaimed king of Mesopotamia, which was renamed Iraq, and set up in a kingdom that would report to Britain. The land that separated Iraq, Syria, and Palestine was labeled "Transjordan," and was handed over to King Hussain's

'Ajman Bedouin (left) and Thalal woman (right), March 13, 1911

other son, Abdullah. He too would govern under an administration that reported to Britain.

And so Abdul Aziz now found himself ruling a portion of land surrounded by unfriendly members of Sharif Hussain's family. And these unfriendly kingdoms all existed under British protection.

The time had come for a new meeting between Abdul Aziz and his old British contact, Percy Cox. The two came together in the winter of 1922, in part to negotiate the boundaries that both sides would agree upon as the limits of the Saudi kingdom. But they were joined by an uninvited guest, a man from New Zealand named Frank Holmes, who initially claimed to be a butterfly hunter seeking a rare variety of black butterfly in the oasis of Qateef.

Frank Holmes was indeed from New Zealand, and he was looking for something rare and black in Qateef, but it was not butterflies. It was oil.

LOST OPPORTUNITIES

When Percy Cox learned of the arrival of the New Zealander, and his real motive, he demonstrated little interest in any meeting with the prospector. Claiming that he and Abdul Aziz were engaged in the far more important matter of settling boundaries, he did his best to discourage Holmes.

Percy Cox was not ignorant of the potential the territory might offer for oil. In fact, quite the opposite. Many of the Middle Eastern regions under British protection were in that position precisely because of their rich oil deposits, and although none had yet been discovered in Arabia, the British had already received hints that some might be found. They had little interest in seeing a non-British contractor move in. Cox went so far as to draft a letter to Holmes, indicating that it would be impossible to agree to give him a concession to look for oil in central Arabia without the approval of the British government. Then he gave the letter to Abdul Aziz and asked him to sign it.

Abdul Aziz was annoyed, but he was also dependent on the annual sum the British government was paying him. He finally agreed to sign the letter, and Frank Holmes left.

But he would be back. A year later, the British government announced that it was ending its policy of giving Arab leaders annual payments. Frank Holmes did not waste any time. Quickly slipping into Arabia, he rushed to Abdul Aziz and presented his own offer for cash in exchange for

Riyadh bazaar, c. 1913–14

the right to prospect in Arabia. Abdul Aziz agreed.

But the story didn't end there. Frank Holmes' group, the Eastern and General Company, did not invest much effort or money in trying to find oil in Arabia. They had obtained the rights to the oil as much to sell it for more money to another oil company as to explore it themselves. The Eastern and General Company believed that a much richer source of oil lay in Bahrain, and so that is where they invested most of their effort. Their investment paid off in 1932, when oil was struck in Bahrain.

The Eastern and General Company stopped their

Well-pit at an oasis near Riyadh, c. 1913–1914

payments to Abdul Aziz in 1927, and so forfeited their rights to oil found there. Little did they realize that they had given up the chance to find the richest source of oil in the world.

These annual payments would determine the course of Arabia's modern history. The Eastern and General's decision to stop their payments opened the door to American oil prospectors in the 1930s, whose discovery of oil would propel the Saudi family to an almost unimaginable fortune, and would spark a relationship between the U.S. and Saudi Arabia that would drastically affect the politics of both countries.

And the decision by the British to stop their payments to Arab leaders—both to Abdul Aziz and Sharif Hussain—

removed the one barrier that had kept the Saudis from attacking the Hejaz region. Abdul Aziz had been dependent on the British cash to keep his kingdom financially afloat, and the threat of its loss (should he attack a British ally) had kept his kingdom confined to the agreed-upon boundaries. But now the money was gone, and Abdul Aziz needed cash. There was one source of steady, annual income in Arabia: the money that came from the international pilgrims who traveled each year to Mecca. The holy city that lay to the south and west of Riyadh each year gathered up vast sums of money in fees and food and lodging.

Abdul Aziz had two choices: preside over yet another downfall of a Saudi kingdom or launch an attack on Sharif Hussain. It did not take him long to decide which option to pursue.

Interior of the mosque, Medina, c. 1907

The 1908 gift catalog of the Royal Geographical Society lists the photographer of this
and the following four photos as Hallajian. The captions are original.

4

Birth of
a Nation

As Abdul Aziz was planning his attack on the Hejaz, Sharif Hussain was focusing on a very different problem—the unexpected loss of support from the British. It was not only the loss of the annual payment that had proved disturbing; it was the clear signs that the British empire was growing ever more distant.

The fault was in part that of the British, whose intelligence had led them to believe that Sharif Hussain's forces were vastly superior to any other army in the region. But the swift and bloody triumph by the Ikhwan at Kurmah had made it clear that their assumptions may have been flawed.

Worse still was the fact that Sharif Hussain was becoming a very difficult and demanding ally. In the earliest days, the British had given him to believe that he would one day become king of all Arabs—a title that he had assumed meant that he would rule over all of Arabia, Iraq, Syria, Lebanon, and Palestine. Of course, the British had no intention of giving control of such a vast territory to one man, and while they had set up his sons in portions of the territory, each region was kept separate and very firmly under British control.

At 71, Sharif Hussain was becoming bitter and angry at how the British had duped him. His moods became unpredictable and he would often react violently, throwing anyone who displeased him into prison.

The loss of the British annual payment meant that he, too, began to search for alternative forms of revenue. His solution: a series of taxes—a water tax, a stamp tax, an income tax—on his own citizens. He also increased the cost of the pilgrimage to Mecca, and banned any form of travel on the pilgrimage except the special camels owned by his own family.

As rumors of Sharif Hussain's instability—and his people's discontent—began to spread, the idea of a more dependable presence in the region became increasingly attractive to the British, in part to protect their own interests in the surrounding countries. They knew that a revolt or instability in the Hejaz could quickly spread to Iraq, to Transjordan, to Palestine. Suddenly, the prospect of Abdul Aziz marching on the holy cities was no longer a move that might have to be blocked by British force. It might instead be a welcome alternative.

THE FINAL STRAW

The end of the reign of Sharif Hussain was sparked by a change not in Arabia, or even Britain, but instead in Turkey. The former political center of the Ottoman

Empire was now in the hands of a modernizing leader named Kemal Atatürk, who had determined that one of the keys to breaking with the Ottoman past was to transform Turkey into a secular (non-religious) state. On May 3, 1924, Sharif Hussain learned that Atatürk had decided to abolish the caliphate—the religious leadership of Islam that had been guarded by the Ottomans for some 400 years. There would be no more caliph in Turkey, and the direction for Muslims throughout the world would no longer come from Constantinople.

The leadership of Islam was "up for grabs," and Sharif Hussain wasted no time. On March 5, 1924, Sharif Hussain announced that, as guardian of the holy cities of Mecca and Medina, he would be the next caliph, the official successor to the prophet Muhammad and leader of all Muslims throughout the world.

Within Hussain's kingdom, the news sparked little reaction. But the announcement made a much greater impression elsewhere. Muslims in other parts of the world suspected a British plot. The British, in turn, expressed their dismay and announced that they would not recognize Hussain's new title. And in the Saudi kingdom, the news sparked great anger—anger that would be turned into opportunity.

CONQUEST OF MECCA

Abdul Aziz understood the opportunity, but he was also well aware of the risks. The conquest of the Hejaz area, the seizing of Mecca and Medina, would drastically change the Saudi empire. Assuming control of the holy cities would, to a devout Muslim like Abdul Aziz, mean a very different kind of responsibility from one he had assumed before. He was comfortable dealing with the Bedouins, and overseeing an empire of desert and settlements.

Nearer view of the tomb at Mada'in Salih, Hejaz, c. 1907

Mada'in Salih had been a Nabataean center on a major trading route. The Nabataeans were a people of ancient Arabia (c. 4th century B.C.–1st century A.D.). The Nabataean script is the ancestor of the Arabic alphabet.

Could he control a more urban community? Did he wish to oversee the extension of the Saudi empire into Mecca and Medina, and take on the mantle of "guardian of the faith" that this would require?

As before, Abdul Aziz's concern centered on his wish to be seen not as conquering Mecca or Medina, but rather as being invited in. And so he called for a gathering of the ulema, of other leaders in his kingdom, and also sent out messengers to Muslims around the world. Abdul Aziz detailed for these leaders the problem posed by Sharif Hussein and requested that the international community of Muslims support a Wahhabi campaign to march into Mecca and force the Sharif to step down.

There was little response to this message from the Saudis, but one of the few that did respond made a critical difference. A representative from the Muslim population of India sent a note giving their support for the campaign. At the time, India was, of course, still a part of the British Empire. With this simple message, the British could be expected not to interfere with any attempt to march on Hejaz. And so, with this final obstacle firmly removed, the Wahhabis prepared for war.

In August of 1924, three months after the annual pilgrimage had ended, 3000 Ikhwan soldiers began their march west toward the town of Taif. Sharif Hussain had been expecting the attack, and the Taif city walls had been fortified and equipped with guards and weapons. But when the Wahhabi warriors arrived, they found little resistance and within three days the city prepared to surrender.

It is not clear what happened next. Some argue that the surrender was not clear and that one side fired upon another. All that is known is that, as the city of Taif surrendered and opened its gates to the Wahhabis, a massacre quickly followed. Everything of value was taken from the helpless citizens, and they were brutally slaughtered. As the violent army prepared to march on to Mecca, panic began to break out among the citizens there, who had heard rumors of the terrible events in Taif. Sharif Hussain pleaded for British assistance, but his request was denied.

The only possible hope lay in the immediate abdication of Sharif Hussain in favor of his son Ali, who might be able to negotiate a better deal with the Saudi forces. Surprisingly, Sharif Hussain agreed, perhaps knowing that without British support he had little hope of withstanding the assault. On the evening of October 3, 1924, he signed the document agreeing to the abdication. Within two weeks, the man who had claimed to be king of all Arabs, who had seized the caliphate and declared himself Muhammad's successor, was fleeing for his life, a flight made somewhat easier by what went with him—several kerosene cans stuffed with hundreds of thousands of dollars in gold coins.

On the same day that Sharif Hussain left Arabia, four members of the Ikhwan army appeared outside the gates of Mecca. The gates were open, but they were the only things open—all of the shops were closed, all windows and doors shut and barred. Almost no one was in Mecca. The news of the massacre at Taif had so frightened the citizens of Mecca that they had closed up their city and left, fleeing into the desert, into nearby cities, wherever they could go to escape the dreaded Ikhwan.

But Abdul Aziz had given strict warnings to his warriors: the holy city was not to be damaged. And so the four Ikhwan who entered the city had dressed themselves in white towels—the traditional garment worn by travelers who came to make the annual pilgrimage—and they had left their weapons behind. They were as defenseless as Mecca itself when they rode into the empty city to declare that it had become part of the Saudi empire.

It would be three long months before Abdul Aziz arrived at Mecca to claim the city, and when he finally arrived, in December of 1924, he was careful to make it clear that a new era had come. He refused to stay in the impressive palace Sharif Hussain had built; instead, he set up camp outside the city walls, took off his robes, and then he too put on the simple white clothes worn by all pilgrims.

With Mecca firmly in his control, Abdul Aziz turned to the other critical parts of the Hejaz: Medina and Jiddah. The siege of these two cities lasted for several months, in part because Abdul Aziz had given instructions to his Ikhwan forces not to utterly destroy the cities, but instead to simply keep up the fighting to force surrender. On the other side, Sharif Hussain's son, Ali, who had inherited what remained of the kingdom, was left to defend the cities in a desperate last stand.

By December of 1925, the last stand was over. Ali left Jiddah, having been promised that he and his family could depart in peace to join his brother Feisal in Iraq and that his citizens would not be subjected to violence from the Ikhwan forces outside the city gates. Both promises were given and the last remaining parts of the Hejaz became part of the Saudi empire.

On January 8, 1926, Abdul Aziz was proclaimed the new king of the Hejaz by the leader of Mecca's Holy Mosque. He had taken back the last piece of the Saudi empire, 24 years after his first victory in Riyadh had marked the beginning of the new age of Saudi leadership in Arabia.

THE FINAL BATTLE

Abdul Aziz had succeeded in winning for himself the kingdoms of Nadj (central Arabia) and the Hejaz. His victory had, in large part, been due to the fearsome fighting of the Ikhwan. The religious fervor that had inspired their willingness to fight to the death had expanded Abdul Aziz's territory. But as so often happens, it also proved difficult to rein in once the need for battle had (in Abdul Aziz's eyes) been eliminated.

The Ikhwan turned their eyes toward Iraq, toward other territories, and saw new lands to conquer and new people to convert. Abdul Aziz was satisfied with the size of his kingdoms and had no wish to spark an international war on the basis of religious motivations. So he faced a new challenge—convincing his fighting force to abandon the principles and the lifestyle that had guided them thus far, and instead assume a more settled existence, one in which Saudi Arabia could begin the process of modernization.

For the Ikhwan, it was an impossible choice. And so, once more, Abdul Aziz had to prepare to fight, but this time against some of the very men who had fought so fiercely on his side only a short time ago. For the first time, the Ikhwan would lose.

Two events firmly shaped the course of the land that would become Saudi Arabia in the early part of the 1930s. Early in 1930, Abdul Aziz arranged a meeting with the ruler of Iraq, King Feisal, the son of his former enemy Sharif Hussain. Abdul Aziz made it clear, through their very public and seemingly friendly encounters, that the era of conflict between the Saudis and members of the Hussain family (known as the Hashemites) had come to an end. His focus would no longer be on extending his empire, but instead on governing it.

The second significant act took place in September 1932, when Abdul Aziz made the announcement that from that date his two kingdoms—the Kingdom of Nadj and the Kingdom of the Hejaz—would be unified and governed as a single land. The new kingdom would be known as Saudi Arabia. Its flag would make clear both its past (two crossed swords) and its future (the palm tree, representing the peaceful and settled life offered by an oasis).

And with this act, Abdul Aziz's campaign to restore the glory of the Saud name had finally succeeded. His new country—Saudi Arabia—extended over a territory as vast

Medina, c. 1907

Photographed by Hallajian.

as that of Western Europe. In little more than 30 years, he had created a kingdom that would become one of the most powerful nations in the world, all because of a treasure that lay below the sand.

AMERICAN PHILANTHROPY

As the 1930s unfolded, Abdul Aziz found himself the ruler of a vast kingdom, but it was a kingdom in need of money. Abdul Aziz had a reputation for generosity—anyone who appeared at his home at mealtimes was fed, and gifts were bestowed liberally and lavishly on the many who thronged around him claiming some need. It was in keeping with the Bedouin custom to share freely what one had, but this policy of giving often and generously had left the Saudi empire impoverished.

It was for this reason that an American philanthropist named Charles R. Crane arrived in the kingdom. Crane came from a wealthy family, and he had served as an advisor to the American president Woodrow Wilson. He was familiar with the Middle East and, more significantly, had proved generous in the past to rulers of Middle Eastern nations.

Crane offered to provide the Saudis with a mining engineer who worked for him, a man named Karl Twitchell, who might help with plans to create a water supply for the city of Jiddah. And so, in the early part of 1931, the thoughts of Abdul Aziz were far from oil, which Frank Holmes had failed to find some 10 years earlier. Instead, he was thinking of something that held far greater value for his people—water.

After several weeks of travel through the Hejaz region, Twitchell returned to Abdul Aziz with discouraging news. He had studied the land carefully, and there were no water resources there. But Abdul Aziz was desperate for potential sources of income, and asked Twitchell to keep looking, in the hope that some other minerals might be found. Twitchell went back to the United States, looking for funding from an oil company that might be willing to support a more extensive exploration of Saudi Arabia's resources, as the kingdom itself had no money to underwrite that expense. But he was turned down.

Abdul Aziz had held, until that point, little interest in oil or its potential revenues. But he soon learned that two of his neighboring rulers—the sheiks of Bahrain and Kuwait—were receiving substantial sums for the rights to dig for oil in their tiny countries. Surely there must be some company, somewhere, that would pay him for the right to look for oil in Saudi Arabia. He went to Twitchell for his advice, and the American gave him some valuable counsel. Wait, the American advised, and see exactly what happens if oil is found.

The answer came in June of 1932. Oil was discovered in Bahrain, by the Standard Oil Company of California (Socal), and with that discovery it seemed very likely that oil also might be found in the al Hasa region of Saudi Arabia, only 25 miles away. Socal came to Abdul Aziz, offering to negotiate through one of his trusted advisers, Harry St. John Philby, while the Iraq Petroleum Company, a consortium owned jointly by British, French, American, and Dutch interests, sent its own British representative to plead its cause. Abdul Aziz ultimately chose Socal, and an agreement was reached granting Socal the right to search for oil in exchange for a substantial sum. Further details specified the amount the company would pay should oil be discovered, and the amount that would be paid for the oil that was drilled. To Abdul Aziz, it was money for nothing. He had been told before that oil might be found beneath the sand, and nothing had been discovered. He held no great confidence that there was anything to the rumors this time, but the money would help to sustain his kingdom.

Much of British motivation, at the time the Middle East was first carved up, was the knowledge that oil would be found, and the choice of lands to place under

Pilgrim fort at Mo'azzam: "The best of the three citadels on the caravan route," c. 1907

Photographed by Hallajian.

mandate was motivated by this knowledge. The desire for oil shaped many of the strategic decisions made by British politicians in the days after World War I, and indeed in Iraq and Kuwait and Bahrain the British had been able to profit from their presence and from the willingness of local rulers to grant them the necessary prospecting concessions. But they did not realize the potential of Saudi Arabia until it was too late. In Saudi Arabia, it was the Saudis—and the Americans—who would most benefit from their mistake.

BLACK GOLD

In 1933, Socal set up its base and began the search for oil. For several years only small traces were found—nothing to support the hope of any major discovery. At one point Abdul Aziz even asked the engineers to dig a few water wells, making it clear that he held far greater hopes for the discovery of a source of water than of oil.

As the prospectors searched for oil, Abdul Aziz searched for a sensible solution to the question that had been troubling him for some time: who would succeed him as ruler of Saudi Arabia? His oldest son, Turki, had died after an illness in 1919. His second son, Saud Ibn Abdul Aziz, was a gregarious and generous man, but he was not the leader that his father had been and, as Abdul Aziz well knew, it had taken him a lifetime to develop the skills to meet so many competing needs and hold together such a vast kingdom. Instead, by the 1930s, he had decided upon a novel solution: the kingdom would be ruled by a kind of committee or consensus, with both Saud and his brother Faisal ruling together, as king and crown prince. By passing the succession from brother to brother, rather than father to son, it was hoped that the family as a whole would gather together to choose the best leader, and it would eliminate the chance of any rivalry that might arise should only one son be selected, who would then retain the power for his family alone.

It is this system that governs Saudi Arabia to this day. The crown prince holds a position nearly as powerful as that of the king, and also serves as an official spokesperson for the royal family. Major decisions are made by a gathering of members of the family leadership, and all benefit when the kingdom prospers. The king and crown prince are selected from those family members deemed best able to lead the country—a choice made with the knowledge that the wealth and power of all the family must be entrusted in the safest and most skillful hands.

With the decision of succession resolved, next came the discovery that would make the entire family very rich indeed. For on March 20, 1938, the five-year quest of Socal (whose name had by now been changed to Casoc) ended. Seven wells had been dug into the rocky soil of Damman Dome, and they had yielded little. Finally, in desperation, a decision was made to extend the seventh well just a bit deeper, and one mile below the earth's surface came the oil that would change nearly everything in Saudi Arabia—oil in seemingly endless supply, oil that would make Saudi Arabia one of the most powerful nations in the world, oil that would make the family of Abdul Aziz rich beyond anyone's imagining.

THE WAGES OF WAR

The discovery of oil made Abdul Aziz a much more significant ally, but this brief period of diplomatic significance would be dimmed by the outbreak of World War II. Oil production ground to a halt, the trip across the Persian Gulf became a hazardous journey, and many of the oil workers returned to their homes.

Abdul Aziz spent the war astutely courting and being courted by both sides. He concluded arms deals with both Germany and Italy, and yet also maintained a strong relationship with the British. Neither side realized that he was negotiating with the other until well after the war had ended, and by then Abdul Aziz had made clear that his sympathies were firmly with the victorious Allied forces. But these sympathies would fade when it became clear that Britain once more intended to shape policy in the Middle East, this time by establishing a Jewish homeland in the Arab land of Palestine.

Abdul Aziz was no supporter of the Nazi Holocaust. What outraged him was the plan to compensate for the horrible actions of a European nation (Germany) by handing over an Arab nation instead. The Arabs of Palestine had not committed the outrages against European Jews, he argued, so why should they be expected to pay the price for them?

By now, the United States had firmly entered the picture. An oil shortage in 1943 had made clear the importance of preserving American access to an oil supply in Saudi Arabia once the war had ended. And so a secret approach was made to Abdul Aziz—would he be willing to meet with the American president, Franklin Roosevelt? He agreed.

On February 14, 1945, at the Great Bitter Lake in the Suez Canal, President Roosevelt welcomed the Saudi king on board the USS *Quincy*. On the agenda: the question of Palestine, and ways to resolve what both sides felt was British mishandling of the problem.

After Roosevelt had outlined the tales of suffering the Jews had experienced, Abdul Aziz offered a simple and straightforward solution: the Jews should be given their choice of the best land, the most impressive homes, of the Germans who had been responsible for their suffering. The conversation moved on to other matters, and in the end, Abdul Aziz believed that Roosevelt had offered his assurance that America would not support the Jews in any aggressive action against the Arabs of Palestine.

His meeting with British leader Winston Churchill, three days later, was less successful. Churchill ignored the Saudi prohibition on smoking and alcohol and consumed both in front of the Saudi king. Further, he had no interest in compromising on the question of the establishment of a Jewish state in Palestine, and instead requested Abdul Aziz's support for the plan, in recognition of the

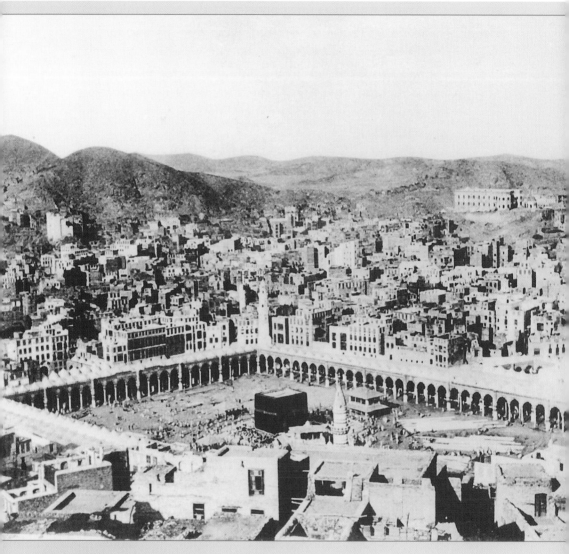

City of Mecca and Ka'ba square, c. 1907

Photographed by Hallajian.

support and friendship Britain had offered throughout the years.

Churchill seems to have been somewhat confused in his facts—Britain had in fact offered little support to Abdul Aziz, and instead had consistently supported his rival. But Abdul Aziz returned home confident in the promises Roosevelt had offered—that Arabs in Palestine would be protected and involved in any decisions about the settlement of their land.

But the promises made by Roosevelt would soon be forgotten, for by April 1945 he was dead and the new U.S. president, Harry Truman, had made his own set of promises: to support the establishment of a Jewish homeland in Palestine.

Ibn Saud, King of Saudi Arabia, c. 1934

5

Death of a Nation Builder

The story of the creation of modern Saudi Arabia begins with Abdul Aziz, but it does not end there. For the history of this important part of the Middle East extends beyond the life and achievements of one man, and reflects the attitudes and actions of his family, as well.

By 1953, Abdul Aziz was nearly 77 years old. He was suffering from arthritis so severe that it had left him crippled and confined to a wheelchair, and he had become nearly blind. A powerful nation had been created, but the man who had made it happen was finding it increasingly difficult to govern it.

On November 9, 1953, Abdul Aziz died, having overseen the restoration of his family's power and honor. The man who had created

Saudi Arabia, in keeping with the practice of his Wahhabi faith, was buried in an unmarked grave in Riyadh. There is no headstone or any sign to mark the final resting place of the man who so drastically altered the history of his homeland.

The story of the son who inherited the Saudi throne, King Saud, offers an example of the best and worst of the kingdom Abdul Aziz had built. In a sense, King Saud was in an impossible position—compared either with the dynamic leader that his father had been, or with the tireless and intelligent manager that his brother would later become. At the beginning of his reign, King Saud constructed a multi-million-dollar palace, complete with swimming pools and mosques. Eleven years later, as his reign was ending in chaos and disarray, he would choose to end his time as king barricaded within those same gaudy walls.

Many of King Saud's accomplishments are overlooked because of the corruption and financial mismanagement that characterized his reign. King Saud was instrumental in emphasizing the importance of Islam within the kingdom. He decided to abolish the annual tax that Muslim pilgrims had traditionally paid for the privilege of visiting Mecca, saying that he could afford to pay the tax for them.

In fact, a generous nature was one of the few traits of his father that King Saud inherited. He was generous to Islamic causes, helped to create welfare facilities, and gave money for hospitals, schools, and new highways. It was not long before King Saud had successfully managed to nearly bankrupt the kingdom with his programs, facilities, and government offices, all designed to improve the life of his people but all terribly expensive to maintain.

The second in line to the throne, Crown Prince Faisal, was the exact opposite of his brother, the king. Saud was tall; Faisal was short and thin. Saud had a large family, with many wives; Prince Faisal had one wife and a small family. King Saud was generous and unwilling to see the difference between the country's income and his own; Prince Faisal was more modest in his expenses and possessions.

Despite, or perhaps because of, these differences, King Saud was a popular king and deemed the best choice to succeed his father. The people appreciated his support of Islamic causes and his generous giving toward programs that would benefit the citizens of Saudi Arabia.

But early on in his regime King Saud demonstrated a weakness in two matters of critical importance for a world leader: business and diplomacy. An attempted shipping deal with the wealthy Greek tycoon Aristotle Onassis drew intense protests from the American oil companies that would be expected to pay for the privilege of using someone else's ships instead of their own. The Americans also feared that once the Saudis had begun the process of taking control of the oil tankers, they might soon move to take control of the oil fields themselves. Their threatened withdrawal of oil revenues was enough to make King Saud change his mind— the kingdom would not fare well without the critical influx of cash the oil fields provided. The deal fell apart, but soon other areas of the kingdom began to fall apart, as well.

The King had grown tired of listening to the often lecturing advice from his brother Faisal and other members of his family, and gradually he removed, one by one, the Council of Ministers that had been created under Abdul Aziz. He found more worthwhile the advice offered by his own sons, his own friends, essentially those who would surround him with compliments rather than complaints.

The transition in leadership that had first seemed orderly began to demonstrate its weaknesses at a particu-larly dangerous time. All over the Middle East, Arabs who were dissatisfied by the corrupt regimes ruling them were being drawn to the charismatic Colonel Gamal Abdul Nasser, who had helped to engineer the overthrow of the Egyptian monarchy in 1952. Nasser's message was that the

Arab people had been artificially divided, by barriers created first by the Ottomans and later by the British and other Western powers. Nasser preached that the Arabs really were one people, and should be united under a single nation—a nation that, not coincidentally, he planned to lead.

Not sensing the personal danger that lay in the course Nasser was outlining, King Saud agreed to Nasser's request that they become partners in this new venture to unify Arabs everywhere. He agreed to help underwrite the cost of Arab newspapers publishing Nasser's message throughout the Middle East, and was happy to welcome the arrival of Egyptian soldiers who would, he was promised, help shape the Saudi army into a more modern fighting force, and Egyptian teachers who came to help staff the new schools King Saud was building. These teachers and soldiers had little understanding of the more traditional Arabian society, and instead their message frequently focused on the growing gap between the many wealthy members of the Saudi family (who continued to increase in numbers and income) and the rest of Arabian society.

King Saud had alienated the Americans once by his proposal to nationalize the oil tankers. Now, his alliance with Nasser posed another threat to Western interests. It was Saudi money that was enabling Nasser to spread his message of Arab unity throughout the Middle East, and Saudi money, some suspected, that also helped finance an Egyptian arms deal with Russia.

The trouble became more serious in July of 1956, when Egypt nationalized the Suez Canal. The Canal was a critical waterway, both for oil shipments and other supplies, and the move also brought down the wrath of Britain, France, and Israel. When war followed, King Saud had little choice but to agree to allow Egyptian planes to use his airfields, and to cut off oil sales to Britain and France. But he was not pleased at the fact that a move that would so seriously jeopardize his

War over the Suez Canal, c. 1956

In 1956 Egypt nationalized the Suez Canal. This waterway was critical for the Saudis, and King Saud was not pleased when this move was taken without consultation with him. The Egyptian border policeman in the picture is patrolling the banks of the canal, riding a camel and carrying an automatic weapon.

country's economy was not at least discussed with him first.

An answer to the problem soon came, in the offer from the U.S. of a stronger partnership, and King Saud agreed to travel to the U.S. to meet President Dwight Eisenhower. The U.S. wanted the right to continue to use Dhahran Airport for an air force post; King Saud wanted more economic and military aid. He received both, plus a new role in the so-called "Eisenhower Doctrine"—the king was to act as a moderating force among other Arab nations, a move that would put him on par with Nasser as an Arab leader.

Nasser wasted no time in turning on his former ally. His radio stations issued daily bulletins outlining the excesses and real or imagined corruption of the Saudi royal family and calling upon all Arabs to overthrow the regime.

BROTHER TO BROTHER

The growing threat to the kingdom gravely concerned the second in line to the throne, Crown Prince Faisal. Faisal had found himself gradually being eased out of any kind of decision-making role. He had been appointed President of the Council of Ministers, but Saud seldom consulted the Council over any important matters.

In fact, Saud recently had promoted several of his sons to important positions within the government, overlooking more senior and better-qualified members of the family. Faisal and others in the family were also concerned that this promotion of Saud's sons meant that he planned to ignore their father's plan for the succession to the throne; that rather than seeing the rule pass from brother to brother, Saud intended to hand power to one of his sons.

Of equal concern were the constant changes in foreign policy. Saud had shifted his alliances so often that other Arab countries had become suspicious of Saudi Arabia and ignored it as they formed their own unions. The alliance and then breakdown of the relationship with Nasser had served little except to prompt the Egyptian leader to call for the overthrow of the monarchy, a call that was finding a willing audience among many Saudi citizens dismayed at their king's excessive spending. Saud was even outspending the vast sums pouring in from oil revenues, and the country was teetering on the brink of bankruptcy.

By March 1958, many of the brothers were meeting

secretly to work out a solution to the troubles facing the kingdom. On March 22 they met with King Saud and presented him with the only possible answer. He could remain as king, but the day-to-day management of the kingdom must be handed over to Crown Prince Faisal. To everyone's surprise, he agreed.

It was the system that Abdul Aziz had loosely defined when he first began to plan for his succession—a system where the strengths and weaknesses of the two brothers could complement, rather than frustrate, each other's actions. Faisal's first action involved establishing control over government spending. He cut back on all but the most critical government expenses, and also severely limited the extra sums that had been available to members of the royal family, over and above their fixed annual allowances.

Faisal's personal example helped make the new cutbacks more acceptable to all. He had no entourage and no bodyguards, and he frequently drove his own car himself rather than use a chauffeur. He worked long hours and kept a simple home in stark contrast to the more lavish palaces of other members of the royal family.

More than anything else, he was always prepared. In August of 1960, the CEO of the world's largest oil company at the time, Esso, announced that they needed to cut their prices and so, in turn, would be paying less for the oil they purchased from Saudi Arabia. Crown Prince Faisal was ready. The price cut would mean a loss of millions of dollars from his carefully prepared budget, just at a time when he was beginning to see some improvements in his country's economic status.

But Faisal had a plan—a plan for a union of oil-producing countries that would be able to stand up to the major oil companies. On September 9, 1960, five countries— Saudi Arabia, Iraq, Iran, Venezuela, and Kuwait—came together in Iraq to plan a new strategy. These five countries controlled approximately 80 percent of the world's oil, and the new organization they formed would be known as the Organization of Petroleum Exporting Countries, or OPEC. Other countries would join OPEC over the years, but at the beginning it was these five nations that took a stand to ensure that oil companies would no longer be able to control the prices of the oil they were exporting.

Key to the success of OPEC was the pledge of unity— that no nation would cut a separate deal with an oil company if it would damage one of the other members of the organization. With this action, oil suddenly became more than a resource—it became a political tool, an asset that could be used to shift the balance of power away from the West and toward the Middle East.

It was a triumph for Arab unity, and a personal triumph for Faisal. Unfortunately, he had enjoyed a few too many triumphs since assuming a more active role in Saudi affairs—balancing the budget, creating economic stability, and now overseeing the creation of a new international entity. King Saud had tired of the ceremonial role, and also tired of the focus on his brother's accomplishments. In December 1960 he announced that he was taking back the full powers of king once again, and also naming himself President of the Council of Ministers.

The move did not cause intense dismay among family members who had been forced to make their own cutbacks under Faisal's campaign of frugality. Some of them had felt that he had not paid sufficient attention to their plans; others felt that he had gone too far.

But within a year King Saud fell gravely ill. Doctors within Saudi Arabia were unable to properly care for him, and it was decided that the only possibility of a cure required him to seek care outside the country. Less than a year after he was unceremoniously demoted, Faisal was back in power again.

Gamal Abdel Nasser, c. 1956

King Saud had an uneasy relationship with Gamal Abdel Nasser, president of Egypt, who was a strong advocate for uniting Arabs across national boundaries. This alliance posed a threat to Western interests and the Saudi Royal Family.

AN OLD FOE

By mid-August of 1962, Nasser had renewed his call for Arabs to overthrow the Saudi family, indicating that Arab attempts to free Jerusalem should only follow Arab attempts to free Riyadh first. One month later, a revolution in neighboring Yemen had ousted the royal family there, and Egyptian forces arrived to cement a revolutionary government and then make plans to carry the revolution north into Saudi Arabia.

These developments were particularly worrying to Crown Prince Faisal, who was once more in the number-two spot. King Saud had returned from medical treatments a few months earlier and had, once more, taken back full power. But the events in Yemen, so close to the Saudi border, were deemed enough of an emergency to prompt the family to insist that Faisal once more be closely involved in the day-to-day running of Saudi Arabia, in part to plan a strategy for possible war.

Faisal quickly cemented an alliance with U.S. President John F. Kennedy. America would provide military support by arranging for joint U.S.–Saudi military exercises. In exchange, Faisal agreed to institute certain reforms in Saudi Arabia—including the abolishment of slavery. This was accomplished by the government itself, which paid for the freedom of all slaves in the kingdom.

It had been a small price to pay for what would prove sufficient military power to repel an Egyptian attack. Nasser's forces had superior weapons (courtesy of their Russian arms trade), but soon American jet fighters were flying over Riyadh and Jeddah, a clear signal that an Egyptian attack would meet not only with Saudi, but also American, resistance.

The threat to Saudi Arabia from an outside force was thus successfully put down, but the internal struggles within the royal family were much more difficult to manage. King Saud simply did not wish to be a king in name only. He began to call upon others for support when he found the ranks of his family closing against him. He turned to tribal leaders, religious leaders, even those who were suspected of supporting Nasser, and this proved the final straw to his exasperated family. Saud had broken the family rule of never showing weakness to outsiders. As the family began to turn against him, King Saud barricaded himself in his royal palace and surrounded it with members of the Royal Guard. In response, other brothers placed the armed forces on high alert, and the National Guard was called out.

It was a tense time, finally resolved at the end of 1963 by King Saud's coming out of his palace and agreeing to allow Faisal to remain in charge, provided that he be allowed to represent Saudi Arabia in the upcoming Arab conference in Cairo. Once more the brothers reached an agreement; once more King Saud forgot the agreement within a few months; and, by March of 1964, Saud was once more demanding to be given back full control of the country.

But this time the outcome was very different. In the last dispute, it had been made clear that Faisal had the full support not only of his family, but of the ulema (the religious leaders) as well. Now the ulema agreed to draw up a *fatwa* (a religious ruling) spelling out that Faisal's powers would be his permanently, and that Saud would serve only as the head of state, and not the ruler.

King Saud was furious, refusing to accept a redefinition of his role to a purely ceremonial one. He insisted that the ulema and the family reconsider their decision. The leading members of the family and leading representatives of the ulema came together and found themselves in total agreement. There could not be a king of Saudi Arabia in name only. King Saud must abdicate, and Faisal must be declared the new king of Saudi Arabia. On November 3, 1964, King Saud agreed to step down and went into exile.

King Faisal of Saudi Arabia, c. 1973

King Saud's brother, Faisal, came back into power in 1962 when his brother fell
gravely ill and had to leave the country for treatment. King Faisal reigned from
1964 to 1975.

6

The Diligent King

King Faisal had demonstrated that his approach to rule was radically different from that of his brother, and he set to work, carving out a precise schedule of long hours, interrupted only by the call to prayer that temporarily halts life in Saudi Arabia five times a day.

His reign lasted from 1964 until 1975, and during that time Faisal's discipline and diligence transformed palace life from indulgent excess to a focus on the family business—the family business being, of course, ruling Saudi Arabia. But it was definitely not business as usual under Faisal's leadership. In the same way that he had quietly and efficiently streamlined Saudi Arabia's economy as crown prince, his time as king was marked by additional domestic reforms, many of these influenced by his wife, Iffat. It was Iffat's focus on educational reform that helped transform what had been a restrictive system of schooling into a more contemporary training. Iffat helped to oversee the introduction of more modern subjects into school studies—things like science and foreign languages—and, perhaps most controversial of all, she helped champion the cause of education for girls. In a country where women live essentially separate lives, where they are not allowed to drive a car or appear in public unveiled, the concept of training them for something better than life in the harem led to intense debate.

While his wife was helping to spark greater opportunities for women's education, Faisal was focusing on the unifying opportunities Islam presented. Faisal saw this as an important check to the revolutionary cries of nationalism championed by Nasser. There was no need, in Faisal's eyes, to create yet another kind of unity for Arabs, when the unity offered by faithful devotion to the tenets of Islam provided a more all-encompassing connection.

Faisal traveled to various nations in the Middle East, Asia, and Africa, calling upon Muslims to unite to form a force that could yield tremendous international influence. The Six-Day War of 1967, in which Israel attacked Syria, Jordan, and Egypt, was a bitter disappointment to King Faisal, resulting in Israel's capture of Jerusalem, a city holy to Muslims as well as to Jewish and Christian believers. But it firmed his resolve that greater ties were needed among the Arab nations, leading to a peacemaking gesture toward the defeated Egyptian President Nasser.

It also marked the beginning of a change in the relationship between Saudi Arabia and the United States. While Nasser had been an enemy, the U.S. had been a valuable ally. But now Nasser's threat had diminished, and the U.S. had become an enthusiastic supporter of Israel. In part, the support of Israel was viewed as a countermove against the supply of Russian arms flowing into Egypt and Syria. But it was a vicious cycle, and one that could be viewed quite differently depending on which side you were on. For the U.S., support of Israel helped to balance the growing Russian presence among the neighboring Arab nations. But as the supply of U.S. arms to Israel increased, its increasingly aggressive stance caused the Arab nations to form their own arms deals to stave off the growing threat from Israel.

CHANGING TIMES

By 1973, Egypt had a new president, Anwar Sadat. He had attempted to carve out some sort of resolution of the growing military buildup, but his tentative efforts at peace-making had been ignored by an American administration focused on Vietnam and the growing conflict there. Sadat and King Faisal shared a reliance on Islam, and also a conviction that the buildup in arms deliveries from the U.S. to Israel would inevitably lead to war.

King Faisal sent a signal to Washington—a message carried by his Oil Minister to leading members of President Nixon's cabinet. It noted the need for the U.S. to call off the rush to increase arms shipments to Israel, or face the consequences. But it was a message that was largely dismissed as an empty threat.

On October 6, 1973, Egypt attacked Israeli forces on the opposite side of the Suez Canal on Yom Kippur, the Jewish Day of Atonement. As the war began to unfold, a meeting was held between members of OPEC and the oil companies. OPEC made it clear that a price increase was needed, essentially doubling the price of oil. By October 12, the talks had broken down, with the oil companies requesting the right to consult their governments before agreeing to such a drastic rise in prices. Their opinion quickly became irrele-vant. The OPEC nations met again on October 17, this time setting the price of oil themselves. It would mark a dramatic change in the way oil companies would do business with Arab nations from then on—with that decision, it became the right of the oil-producing countries, rather than the companies, to set the price of their oil.

King Faisal was not happy, but he did not want to cripple the United States. He decided that a small cut-back in production was in order—just enough to send the message that the OPEC nations meant business. The message was not received. President Richard M. Nixon determined to increase the amount of aid previously agreed upon for Israel, from $850 million to $2.2 billion.

It was a sum of money that would drastically turn the tide of the war in Israel's favor. But would prove an expensive decision, in more ways than one. On October 19, 1973, King Faisal received the news of the American action. And on that day, he declared *jihad*, or holy war, on the United States. All shipments of oil were to stop immediately.

A NEW POWER

The oil embargo had a drastic impact on life in the United States and Japan and throughout the West. Those who had underestimated the power of a Saudi king suddenly understood how dramatically dependence on oil had shifted the balance of global power. By 1974, a new round of diplomacy had brought an end to the embargo, with the promise of the delivery of U.S. tanks, naval ships, and fighter aircraft to Saudi Arabia.

Suddenly, investment was everywhere. The new price of oil had brought untold revenue to the country and presented it with a problem—how to spend all the money. There were plenty of businessmen eager to offer a solution, and soon cars and consumer goods were pouring into the country.

The money made many Saudis happy, but King Faisal

Grave of King Faisal, March 25, 1975

King Faisal was killed by his nephew, Faisal ibn Musaid, in the royal palace. Apparently, the shooting was not politically motivated, but rather the act of an unstable young man. On March 28, 1975 these Saudi Arabian men visited the site of Faisal's grave on the outskirts of Riyadh.

was not one of them. He had taken the steps he had taken not to become wealthy, but out of a profound belief that he was doing the right thing. He did not like the way that this sudden rush of riches was transforming his country and its people. But he did not have long to worry about the changed status of the land he ruled.

For on the morning of March 25, 1975, the king's 26-year-old nephew, Faisal ibn Musaid, walked into his uncle's palace and joined a delegation from Kuwait who had come to meet with the king. When they walked in, so did he, and as the king reached out to greet his nephew, the young man pulled out a pistol and fired it three times. King Faisal died only a short while later.

No one really understood what had prompted the young man to assassinate his uncle. The truth seemed to be a mixed-up collection of small details: the young man had been mentally unstable; he had been drinking the night before; his younger brother had been killed 10 years earlier, and he felt the king was responsible. There were few answers.

Many would remember the reign of King Faisal as the high point of the Saudi empire. He had transformed Saudi life, while clinging to traditional values. He had made his nation an international power, yet preserved the influence and prestige of the monarchy at a time when Arab nations all around him were falling victim to Nasser's nationalist movement. He had held the kingdom together at its weakest moment, and made it a power that was both respected and feared.

A NEW ERA

King Faisal's death, while unexpected, did not plunge the monarchy into chaos. The system of succession had been established and so the transfer of power was orderly. With the blessing of both the Saudi family and the ulema, the 63-year-old Khalid became king, and his brother Fahd became crown prince.

The king who came to power in 1975 was a moderate who had little experience in politics. To some, his poor health at the time he became king meant that he would only serve briefly, and initially it was felt that the two brothers—the old-fashioned Khalid and the more modern Fahd—would mirror the relationship of Saud and Faisal. But the truth proved more subtle. The system by which the family governs, and the decisions about who will inherit the throne and who will be second and third in line, are considered carefully and, in some sense, designed to provide checks and balances. Crown Prince Fahd was known for his pro-Western stance, but third in line to the throne was his brother

Abdullah, who was known for his anti-American attitudes and support of Arab nationalist leaders. In this way, the Saudi family ensured that no one member could swing the country too far in one direction or the other.

But a system designed to check unlimited power can result in splits and disagreements, and this is what began to emerge in the late 1970s. By 1977, much of the kingdom's economic problems had been solved by the influx of investment and cash for oil. The citizens were leading an increasingly modern life—a fact that disturbed the ulema, who feared that the Saudi family was abandoning its Wahhabi principles and guiding the country astray. King Khalid's health was a concern, it was clear that a new king would soon inherit the throne, and a split was developing between those who supported Prince Fahd's pro-Western stance and those who supported Prince Abdullah's more Arab-oriented views.

International events highlighted the important gap between the two princes' positions. In 1978, the monarchy of the Shah of Iran (a close ally of the U.S.) was overthrown by Shiite fundamentalists. This revolution sparked tremendous concern in Saudi Arabia. Then, in March 1979, the Camp David Accords between President Sadat of Egypt, U.S. president Jimmy Carter, and Menachem Begin of Israel sparked renewed focus on the question of Palestine, and particularly what the Saudi position would be. The pro-Western stance of Crown Prince Fahd suddenly seemed a dangerous position to assume, and facing the prospect of their own overthrow should they link themselves too closely with the West, the Saudi family determined that it was a good time for Crown Prince Fahd to leave the country for a while. During this extended "vacation," Prince Abdullah and others changed the foreign policy of Saudi Arabia, choosing to sever many of their diplomatic ties with the U.S. and instead develop firmer links to other Arab nations, joining in a boycott of Egypt and raising oil prices.

To many, this confused change in foreign policy, the uncertainty generated by the question of King Khalid's poor health, and the internal disagreement within the family, meant that the Saudi monarchy was in its final days. A crisis in Mecca would further challenge the family's resolve and its position.

THE MECCA REBELLION

On the night of November 19, 1979, a young man named Juhayman ibn Muhammad ibn Sayf al Utaybi entered the grounds of the Grand Mosque in Mecca—a shrine viewed by Muslims as the holiest place in the world. He was not alone. With him were nearly 500 followers, and they were equipped with supplies of food and an arsenal of weapons. Early the next morning—a date that marked the beginning of a new year in the Muslim calendar—they stormed the doors of the mosque, firing their rifles and shooting at anyone who blocked their way. They quickly seized control of the Grand Mosque and barricaded themselves inside.

The young man who led the rebellion and his followers were supporters of a kind of neo-Ikhwan philosophy. They believed that the Saudi family had led the country astray with its modernization and the rapid increase in wealth. They preached the need for a return to the traditional values, the old way of life, and believed that they had in their midst the new *Mahdi*, or Messiah, who would lead the country away from its old, corrupt ways and on to a life lived in keeping with the traditional teachings.

For the Saudi family, this event was a disaster. They had claimed for themselves the title of Protector of the Holy Places; the seizure of the Grand Mosque was a direct failure. Police surrounded the temple, but King Khalid was initially uncertain about how best to proceed. The Koran specifically prohibited any desecration of a mosque. Not only would it be a sin to kill a person there; the Koran dictated that not even

The Grand Mosque in Mecca

This shrine, viewed by Muslims as the holiest site in the world, was invaded by men who barricaded themselves inside. The possibility of desecrating or destroying the mosque made for a delay in how the royal family reacted. It was two weeks before the rebels could be convinced to surrender. Thus, during this time these rebels commanded an audience for their call for a more conservative religious path for the nation.

animals or plants could be destroyed within the holy grounds. For this reason, the army or police could not simply fight their way in and overpower the terrorists.

King Khalid requested a meeting with the ulema and asked their permission for the government to shoot if necessary in order to win back the Mosque. Permission was granted. But the Saudi army still needed to be careful to ensure that the Mosque was not seriously damaged or, worse, destroyed. It took two weeks before the rebels finally surrendered, and not before many people had died in the effort.

The royal family was damaged by the ability of the terrorists to seize the Grand Mosque in the first place, and by their inability to quickly suppress this revolt. While criticism was strong against the terrorists for their actions—shooting guns and killing people on holy ground—the group's denunciations of the royal family and their calls for a return to more conservative religious values touched a nerve. As a result, both King Khalid and Crown Prince Fahd began to delegate more authority to the ulema to oversee religious and moral aspects of life in Saudi Arabia, to ensure that the push to modernize did not abandon traditional Wahhabi ways.

A STRUGGLE FOR POWER

King Khalid's reign ended with his death in June 1982 after a long series of health problems. Crown Prince Fahd became the new king, and Prince Abdullah was named Crown Prince. Although the prearranged succession gave the appearance of proceeding smoothly, the differences that had distinguished Fahd and Abdullah grew more pronounced as they assumed the most senior positions in the kingdom. Abdullah still opposed the pro-Western tilt of the new king's policies. He also resented the fact that he, in the number-two position in the country, would have far less power than his brother had had when he'd served as crown prince. During much of King Khalid's reign, his ill health had forced Fahd to take over the day-to-day administration of Saudi Arabia. Abdullah knew that his own position as crown prince would involve less authority.

Concerned by the rise of Islamic fundamentalist movements throughout the Arab world, Fahd underscored the importance of the ulema, whose position had been strengthened considerably by the siege at Mecca. King Fahd met weekly with the religious leaders, consulting them to ensure that the pace of modernization did not radically interfere with the *Shari'a*, the Islamic law that is the basis for judicial decisions in Saudi Arabia.

These steps would win back some public support, but the regime was confronted by a new group of dissatisfied citizens—a growing middle class that was well-educated and that had experienced prosperity. They had no wish to go back to the old days, and they were increasingly dissatisfied by the presence of a royal family that seemed to grow increasingly wealthy and powerful at a time when jobs and opportunities were no longer plentiful for the rest of the country.

As the 1980s unfolded, there was a sense that the good times were ending for Saudi Arabia, and perhaps for its rulers. The question was, what would come next? Would Saudi Arabia choose to side with the Arab nations whose own monarchies had been overthrown by radical movements? Or would it choose to move closer to Western nations?

The choice was made clearer in August 1990, when the leader of Iraq sent his troops into Kuwait and then turned his sights on the Saudi borders.

General Colin Powell and Operation Desert Storm, c. 1990

Colin Powell (left), chairman of the Joint Chiefs of Staff, surveys a Marine position in Saudi Arabia near the border with Kuwait. Powell was in Saudi Arabia to meet with the troops and discuss military affairs with other American and Saudi commanders.

7

A Storm in the Desert

From 1980 until 1988, the countries of the Middle East had witnessed a bitter war between Iraq and Iran. The Saudis, the Kuwaitis, and several other nations (including the U.S.) had supported Iraqi leader Saddam Hussein's efforts to combat the revolutionary regime in Iran. But when the war finally ended, both the Saudi and Kuwaiti governments looked for their debt to be repaid. This outraged Saddam Hussein, who felt that he had helped combat the spread of Iran's brand of revolutionary Islam on behalf of all of the neighboring Middle Eastern countries.

Saddam Hussein had little interest in repaying his debts at a time when the post-war Iraqi government was experiencing economic troubles. Ultimately he had a very different plan in mind. On August 2, 1990, an army of 100,000 Iraqi troops and 300 tanks rolled across the border. The Kuwaiti army, a mere 16,000 men, was no match for this invasion force. The Kuwaiti emir (the royal ruler of the tiny country) and his family fled their land, and the Kuwaiti armed forces quickly surrendered.

The invasion, and the clear indication that Saudi Arabia would be the next target of the Iraqi forces, prompted a swift reaction. At the heart of the U.S.–Saudi relationship had been a basic understanding—Saudi Arabia provided the oil, while the U.S. promised the security. With Iraqi troops marching across Kuwait toward Saudi Arabia, the time had come to focus on the "security" part of the relationship.

Within only a few months, some 500,000 American soldiers were dispatched to Saudi Arabia, preparing for a military campaign that would be known as Operation Desert Storm. The agreements that led to this massive deployment of American troops in the kingdom were not formalized documents, but instead the work of extensive and detailed diplomatic meetings. While the clear short-term goal was to force the Iraqis to withdraw from Kuwait (and ensure that they didn't invade Saudi Arabia), the specific length of time for which U.S. troops would be deployed in Saudi Arabia was never clarified. It was understood that they would remain for as long as it took—but this vague understanding would cause concern in the future when years had passed and several thousand U.S. soldiers still remained stationed on Saudi soil.

Part of the criticism was based in the religion that has guided so much of Saudi political decisions. More conservative Muslims felt that it was a violation of their religious views to have foreign solders permanently based in the home of their holiest shrines.

The Allied forces quickly proved victorious. But while the Saudis were able to protect their country from invasion, they were less successful in their efforts to prevent an economic crisis. Oil prices fell throughout the 1990s, causing a steady decrease in Saudi income. Deficits in the budget became common, and the Saudis' initial willingness to cover the cost of American troops in Saudi Arabia became reluctance as the presence of foreign troops began to pose a public-relations problem.

NEW POLITICS FOR A NEW AGE

The years 1995 and 1996 were marked by twin attacks in Saudi Arabia, this time against American targets. Both were locations heavily populated by American solders. The first took place in Riyadh, and four men were quickly rounded up who confessed to the bombing. They claimed that their actions had been inspired by Osama bin Laden, the son of a wealthy Saudi businessman with links to the royal family who had been preaching an anti-American message from locations throughout Central Asia, the Middle East, and even Africa. The men were swiftly beheaded.

The second attack took place in Dharan, at the Khobar Towers where many servicemen had been based. Again, it became clear that there was a connection to Saudi fundamentalists. In total, 24 Americans were killed in the two incidents, and the U.S. responded by relocating its personnel to a more remote location in the desert.

As the 1990s drew to a close, King Fahd's health began to fail. He had suffered a stroke in 1995, and his health had become an increasing concern. As his brothers had done before, Crown Prince Abdullah stepped forward. Once more there would be a king as figurehead; once more the day-to-day management and running of the country would be handled by the heir to the throne.

A GLIMPSE INTO THE FUTURE

To the surprise of many who forecast its demise decades earlier, the Saudi monarchy outlasted the 20th century. But it is a different empire from that first put together by Abdul Aziz, marked by great contradictions and even greater challenges.

The country that holds approximately one-fourth of the world's oil reserves has become a political force in the Middle East. But its population is growing quickly, far outdistancing the ability of even the most progressive regime to respond with employment opportunities. At the same time, falling oil prices have meant that income is in fact declining—creating a frightening combination of more and more people with less and less money.

The increasing number of young people, many of them well-educated but with few job prospects, has spread a sense of discontent through the streets of Riyadh and other Saudi cities. These are the conditions that provide opportunity for extremists, and there has been great concern in recent years about the swift spread of more radical Islamic elements in Saudi Arabia, preaching an anti-Western, anti-monarchist philosophy. The increasing influence of the ulema has contributed to the imbalance, by placing greater emphasis on educating clerics at the Islamic universities, few of whom can find jobs in mosques, and by stressing religious instruction in schools rather than the technical skills that can provide a better-trained employee. Saudi Arabia has also contributed to the spread of Wahhabism throughout much of the Islamic world by funding religious schools that preach a doctrine of intolerance.

It is interesting that when Crown Prince Abdullah began to assume more of the day-to-day management of his country, his traditional anti-American biases began to soften. When the United States was attacked by terrorists

U.S. Defense Secretary Donald Rumsfeld, October 3, 2001

Shortly after the terrorist attacks on the United States on September 11, 2001, Defense Secretary Rumsfeld (left) embarked on a trip to Saudi Arabia to talk with King Fahd (right) in an effort to strengthen support in the Islamic world for President Bush's campaign against terrorism.

on September 11, 2001, and it became clear that many of the terrorists were Saudis answering to the former Saudi Osama bin Laden, Crown Prince Abdullah did not hesitate. He decided to reverse an earlier OPEC decision to cut oil production, and instead quickly authorized the rapid delivery of additional oil to the U.S.—a decision that in the short-term provided U.S. consumers with less expensive gasoline and in the long-term demonstrated Saudi Arabia's alliance with the United States.

But the challenges—both to the Saudi–U.S. relationship and to the royal family—will continue as the 21st century unfolds. Ongoing concern exists about the Israeli–Palestinian conflict, and how best it should be resolved. Additional concerns focus on the perceived threat posed by other nations in the Middle East and on precisely what sort of U.S. military presence in the kingdom is warranted.

Age is a concern that also confronts the Saudi family. The sons of Abdul Aziz, the traditional heirs to the Saudi throne, are now old men. While one of Abdullah's brothers, Sultan, has already been named to be his successor, time may change the plans for succession as the crown prince and his successor enter their 80s. A power struggle within the royal family may become inevitable.

The politics of modern Saudi Arabia has largely been based on three focal points: Islam, security, and oil. As the modern Middle East took shape around it, the kingdom remained true to its position as guardian of the holy cities of Mecca and Medina, while enjoying the benefits of oil and the security it could buy. But in the 21st century, these three points are enjoying a less peaceful coexistence. The politics that brings security and the wealth that oil provides, can come into conflict with the more austere framework of the Wahhabi faith.

The empire that Abdul Aziz shaped out of desert sand is now a world power, and his sons have become some of the wealthiest men in the world. The past is still clearly visible in Saudi Arabia. But the future of the kingdom is far from certain.

Gallery of Photographs
from Saudi Arabia

Gertrude Bell (1868–1926)

Gertrude Bell, an English traveler and explorer and a prolific writer, was instrumental in determining the borders of the new nation of Iraq and in choosing its first ruler, Prince Feisal I (1921). For years, she was his closest personal and political adviser, a position that earned her the title of "Uncrowned Queen of Iraq."

However, dating back to 1899, Bell had explored ancient caravan routes across the deserts of the Middle East. In 1913–14, she explored ancient routes across the Arabian desert westward to the Rashid family stronghold of Ha'il. By the 1890s, Ha'il had become the undisputed capital of all of desert Arabia. At first, Bell was favorably received by the Rashid family. However, when she announced that she planned to visit Ibn Saud, their political enemy, she was detained for ten days as a possible spy and then ordered to Baghdad and out of Arabia.

The following five unique photographs were taken by Gertrude Bell on March 7, 1914 in Ha'il, about seven years before the Saudi conquest of this area.

The Wall, Ha'il, March 7, 1914

These men were sent by the Rashid family to escort Bell toward Baghdad—thus, ending her attempt to go further south in the Arabian desert to meet Ibn Saud. Photographed by Gertrude Bell.

Well, Ha'il, March 7, 1914

Photographed by Gertrude Bell.

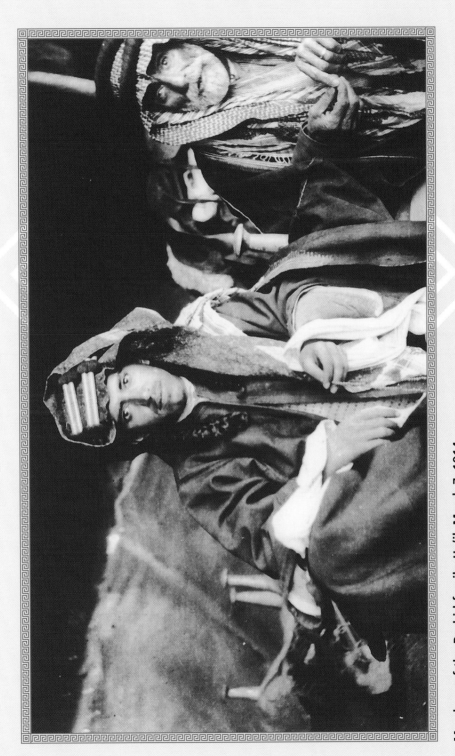

Members of the Rashid family, Ha'il, March 7, 1914

Photographed by Gertrude Bell.

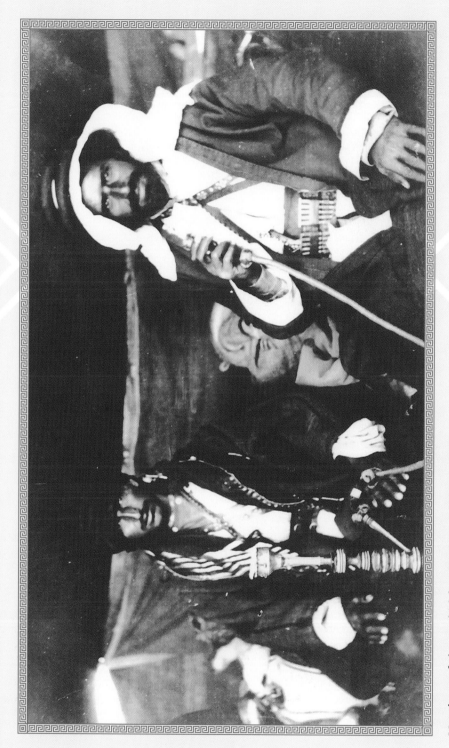

Members of the Rashid family, Ha'il, March 7, 1914

Photographed by Gertrude Bell.

Children, Ha'il, March 7, 1914
Photographed by Gertrude Bell.

1902 Abdul Aziz (Ibn Saud) conquers Riyadh

1914 Sykes-Picot Treaty signed

1921 Cairo meeting held; Middle East divided and rulers appointed

1924 Mecca conquered by Saudi army

1932 Kingdoms of Nadj and the Hejaz unified and new kingdom of Saudi Arabia created

1938 Oil discovered at Damman Dome

1953 Death of Abdul Aziz

1960 OPEC is formed

1964 King Saud abdicates; Faisal becomes king

1973 King Faisal launches oil embargo against U.S.

1975 King Faisal assassinated; Khalid becomes king

1979 Terrorists seize Grand Mosque at Mecca

1982 King Khalid dies; Fahd becomes king

1990 Saddam Hussein invades Kuwait and threatens Saudi Arabia

1991 Gulf War begins

1995 King Fahd suffers stroke; Crown Prince Abdullah assumes more day-to-day management of kingdom

Howarth, David. *The Desert King*. New York: McGraw Hill, 1964.

Lacey, Robert. *The Kingdom*. New York: Harcourt Brace Jovanovich, 1981.

Mackey, Sandra. *The Saudis*. Boston: Houghton Mifflin, 1987.

Stewart, Desmond. *T.E. Lawrence*. New York: Harper & Row, 1977.

WEBSITES

www.countrywatch.com

www.saudiembassy.net

www.arabnews.com

www.saudinf.com

Abir, Mordechai. *Saudi Arabia in the Oil Era*. Boulder, Colorado: Westview Press, 1988.

Al-Farsy, Fouad. *Modernity and Tradition: The Saudi Equation*. New York: Kegan Paul Interntional, 1990.

Doughty, Charles M. *Travels in Arabia Deserta*. New York: The Heritage Press, 1953.

Howarth, David. *The Desert King*. New York: McGraw Hill, 1964.

Lacey, Robert. *The Kingdom*. New York: Harcourt Brace Jovanovich, 1981.

Mackey, Sandra. *The Saudis*. Boston: Houghton Mifflin, 1987.

Stewart, Desmond. *T.E. Lawrence*. New York: Harper & Row, 1977.

Wallach, Janet. *Desert Queen*. New York: Anchor Books, 1996.

Wilson, Jeremy. *Lawrence of Arabia*. New York: Atheneum, 1990.

WEBSITES

www.arabnews.com

www.cia.gov

www.countrywatch.com

www.hejileh.com/countries/saudi.html

www.saudiembassy.net

www.saudinf.com

www.spa.gov.sa

www.washingtonpost.com

Cover: Kurt Stier/Corbis
Frontispiece: Royal Geographical Society

page:

16: Courtesy of the U.S. Central Intelligence Agency. Available through the website at University of Texas at Austin.
17: Courtesy of the U.S. Central Intelligence Agency. Available through the website at University of Texas at Austin.
87: AP/World Wide Photos

91: AP/World Wide Photos
95: AP/World Wide Photos
98: AP/World Wide Photos
110: AP/World Wide Photos
107: AP/World Wide Photos
103: AP/World Wide Photos
115: Associated Press, The Saudi Press Agency

Unless otherwise credited the photographs in this book are from the Royal Geographical Society Picture Library. Most are being published for the first time.

The Royal Geographical Society Picture Library provides an unrivaled source of over half a million images of the peoples and landscapes from around the globe. Photographs date from the 1840s onwards on a variety of subjects including the British Colonial Empire, deserts, exploration, indigenous peoples, landscapes, remote destinations, and travel.

Photography, beginning with the daguerreotype in 1839, is only marginally younger than the Society, which encouraged its explorers to use the new medium from its earliest days. From the remarkable mid-19th century black-and-white photographs to color transparencies of the late 20th century, the focus of the collection is not the generic stock shot but the portrayal of man's resilience, adaptability and mobility in remote parts of the world.

In organizing this project, we have incurred many debts of gratitude. Our first, though, is to the professional staff of the Picture Library for their generous assistance, especially to Joanna Wright, Picture Library Manager.

HEATHER LEHR WAGNER is a writer and editor. She earned an M.A. in government from the College of William and Mary and a B.A. in political science from Duke University. She is the author of several books for teens on global and family issues. She is also the author of *Iran, Iraq*, *The Kurds* and *Turkey* in the Creation of the Modern Middle East series.

AKBAR S. AHMED holds the Ibn Khaldun Chair of Islamic Studies at the School of International Service of American University. He is actively involved in the study of global Islam and its impact on contemporary society. He is the author of many books on contemporary Islam, including *Discovering Islam: Making Sense of Muslim History and Society,* which was the basis for a six-part television program produced by the BBC called *Living Islam.* Ahmed has been a visiting professor and the Stewart Fellow in the Humanities at Princeton University, as well as a visiting professor at Harvard University and Cambridge University.